I0800428

Praise for *Building Together: Collaborative Leadership in Early Childhood Systems* by Fiona Stewart

"Stewart shines a light on the complex web of systems that affect how well young children are served and the nature and characteristics of the leaders who make those systems work. This book is for people who play a leadership role in serving children—and those who want to."

—Gerrit Westervelt, director, early childhood policy and resource development, WestEd; former executive director, BUILD Initiative

"Just as we teach children to collaborate, cooperate, and play well together, Fiona Stewart has provided a pathway for grown-ups to do the same. This includes the all-important step of planning for the inclusion of the 'meaningful voice' of diverse stakeholders. Building together, we can make a change!"

—Debra Ren-Etta Sullivan, cofounder and president of the Praxis Institute for Early Childhood Education and author of *Learning to Lead*

"*Building Together* is a page-turner for ECE practitioners and policymakers alike! With clear reasons why we need to collaborate; leadership models and strategies that inspire us; and rich, real-life examples to show how this works, we can read and continue to consult this book for years to come. Fiona Stewart has given us a golden primer for both beginning and seasoned ECE advocates collaborating for local, regional, state, and national ECE systems change and integration."

—Jan Fish, EdD, co-lead consultant, Partnerships for Education, Articulation and Coordination through Higher Education (PEACH); professor emerita, California State University, Northridge

Building Together

Building Together

Collaborative Leadership in Early Childhood Systems

FIONA STEWART

Redleaf Press®
www.redleafpress.org
800-423-8309

Published by Redleaf Press
10 Yorkton Court
St. Paul, MN 55117
www.redleafpress.org

First edition 2019
Cover design by Jim Handrigan
Cover photograph by istock.com/DESKCUBE
Author photograph by Michael E. Stern
Interior design by Jim Handrigan
Typeset in Minion Pro
Printed in the United States of America
25 24 23 22 21 20 19 18 1 2 3 4 5 6 7 8

Library of Congress Cataloging-in-Publication Data

Names: Stewart, Fiona (Fiona Elaine), author.
Title: Building together : collaborative leadership in early childhood systems / by Fiona Stewart.
Description: First edition. | St. Paul, MN : Redleaf Press, 2018. | Includes bibliographical references and index.
Identifiers: LCCN 2018009272 (print) | LCCN 2018031937 (ebook) | ISBN 9781605545950 (ebook) | ISBN 9781605545943 (pbk. : acid-free paper)
Subjects: LCSH: Early childhood education—Planning. | Early childhood teachers—Professional relationships. | Educational leadership.
Classification: LCC LB1139.23 (ebook) | LCC LB1139.23 .S74 2018 (print) | DDC 372.21—dc23
LC record available at https://lccn.loc.gov/2018009272

Printed on acid-free paper

MIX
Paper from responsible sources
FSC www.fsc.org
FSC® C011935

Contents

Acknowledgments

AS WITH MOST ENDEAVORS, this book was a journey supported by many people in my life.

I first want to acknowledge all those who took time from their busy days to speak with me and share their leadership stories. These include Lea Austin, Liza Bray, Chris Amirault, Neva Bandelow, Jolene Smith, Tanya Palmer, and Michelle Gross. Thanks also to Gerrit Westervelt for his input and for encouraging me to write this and to both him and Judy Sanchez for providing feedback on early ideas.

I also want to thank the editors and staff at Redleaf Press for their support, guidance, and assistance in seeing this through to completion, including Kara Lomen, Kari Cornell, Josh Plattner, Jim Handrigan, and Meredith Burks.

My leadership journey has been one of collaboration, growth, and continued learning. There are many people who have inspired me through the years and whose wisdom and support have been invaluable along the way. My thanks to you all for your leadership, friendship, and mentoring.

This is a field full of challenges and opportunities. My appreciation and gratitude to all who are working every day with and on behalf of children and families and striving for improved systems and resources. I know how hard you work so that we may all do right by the children and families we serve, and I hope this book helps move our field forward.

Thank you to my personal friends both near and far who provided ongoing encouragement.

And most of all, thanks to my son for being the biggest inspiration in my life.

INTRODUCTION

Systems Building in an Increasingly Complex World

SYSTEMS BUILDING refers to all the efforts carried out to create a coordinated and structured approach to delivering programs and services. It is the process that transforms the delivery of direct services and the necessary infrastructure into an organized system. Systems building includes attempts to work across agencies, organizations, sectors, service areas, and even funding streams and purposes. This process can occur at the local, regional, state, or national level.

Throughout the early childhood education (ECE) field, systems work is increasing as communities strive to improve or better align programs and services. The ECE field is a natural fit for collaborative systems-building projects. The focus on helping children learn, providing families with support, fostering relationships, integrating services, and positively affecting communities provides ample opportunities for collaboration, systems alignment, and integration. Sometimes it takes multiple stakeholders working together to best serve a child, family, or community.

That said, collaborative work isn't always easy, especially in ECE and related fields, where the most common mode of operation has been to work in silos. But today more than ever, there is a need for families to receive multiple services in a coordinated fashion. There is a greater focus at the national, state, and local level on the importance of ECE, brain development, educational outcomes and inequities, and the importance of strengthening families.

With this focus, agencies, organizations, and institutions must work more collaboratively and effectively to align, build, or change systems.

Across the country, local communities and states have received funds from different sources for systems-building efforts. This support aims to increase infrastructure, align and link programs, and deliver more efficient, effective, and seamless services to children and families. Many communities have dedicated task forces, work groups, or advisory boards committed to working together to develop comprehensive and integrated early learning systems.

Working Together to Attain Goals

The focus on ECE means there is an even greater need for strong leaders and comprehensive systems-building approaches that address quality, outcomes, and educational inequities. Systems development efforts have increased with the need for greater coordination and improved infrastructure. ECE is a very fragmented field, divided across multiple political and administrative authorities. Among these different departments, programs, and funding sources, various approaches exist. Quality rating and improvement systems (QRIS) and professional development systems are two such approaches, and both offer many opportunities for collaboration.

In addition, the ECE field is often underfunded, leaving fewer resources to address significant social issues. Through collaboration, organizations can leverage a variety of services and funds to help reach target populations or address specific issues. Sometimes it is more cost-effective for an organization to work with other groups to offer programs or services than to try to do it all on its own.

Accomplishing More with Less

Over the past several years, the work of nonprofits and the ECE field has changed dramatically. The recession of 2008 resulted in severe budget cuts in both the private and public sectors. Many agencies and government departments had to rethink how to operate with fewer resources. For some, it was a time to examine new ways to sustain business and identify other sources of revenue. But scarce resources also led to more competition between agencies. As agencies hunkered down to sustain existing funding sources, they looked for creative ways to adapt to the new, more fiscally restrictive climate. Some systems-building efforts rose out of this need to innovate in order to stay afloat and continue to offer services.

The internet has also affected the way we all do business. Families have the benefit of greater access to information, yet there is so much more information to process and try to understand. Through online sources, parents can conduct their own research and voice opinions on possible quality services. The internet empowers families to seek greater access to these services and request that agencies hold themselves accountable to higher standards. This demand now moves at the speed of the internet and social media, yet it doesn't include the warmth of person-to-person contact. In addition to finding ways to provide a sense of connection, build relationships, and offer assistance, organizations need to be able to respond quickly and efficiently with information and solutions.

The Need for Strong Leadership

We need inspired leaders to continue to champion this work. Families struggle with the high cost of care while child care teachers and providers attempt to make ends meet on low wages. To better address the complex challenges today's families face, communities have begun to develop more integrated, strength-based family services. City, county, and state governments are juggling budget demands, system inefficiencies, the economic impact of having both parents in the workforce, and the long-term economic consequences of an inadequate child care system. Effective leadership is critical to building successful, collaborative systems. Additionally, leadership models are needed to support leaders as they initiate, champion, and sustain this work.

Although some may come to this work with natural leadership qualities, the skills and abilities needed to lead successfully can be learned and strengthened over time. With each passing year of reflection and experience, leadership skills grow and become more refined. My own leadership experience has been a journey of continually seeking out ways to make an impact and to effect change in ECE systems, from the classroom level to the state level. I believe that we can better serve the children and families in this country, and every day I strive to do my part. With so much at stake, how we do this work matters. Over the years, I've learned that collaboration is essential to progress. Building and maintaining relationships is crucial; working together toward a common vision is truly beneficial to the community.

Answering the Call

Are you ready to take new steps in your own leadership development? Does systems-building work resonate with you? Why and how might you, an organization, or a community embark on this work? What leadership knowledge and skills are necessary to work collaboratively and shepherd this work through to the end goal? This book will answer these questions and provide guidance on how to successfully lead collaborative efforts and navigate through systems-building work. I've drawn upon real-life examples and lessons learned during my years of experience in collaborative systems building to further enhance the text. Let's get started.

Part I

Leadership for Systems Building

CHAPTER 1

Why Systems-Building Leadership Is Needed

INCREASED FOCUS on the importance the early years play in children's development and the positive role quality early childhood programs have on children's success in school and life has led to renewed efforts to improve the field. From the local level to the state and national level, new funding has created opportunities for innovative programs.

For example, some local communities have created funding to allow the early childhood education (ECE) field to build stipend or coaching programs. At the national level, the Race to the Top—Early Learning Challenge grant helped states build quality rating and improvement systems (QRIS) aimed at enhancing the ECE system. With this greater focus on ECE, the need for more coordination and improved infrastructure has provided the opportunity to improve or better align programs and services.

In addition, local organizations and communities continue to seek ways to address the many challenges facing children and families. For children to thrive, communities may need to think comprehensively and systemically to provide workable solutions to common problems. Poverty, homelessness, health and nutrition, literacy, foster care, mental health, disabilities, trauma, and more affect children each day in and around their ECE settings. Working together creates ways to coordinate services that can lift up the whole family and increase a child's opportunities for success.

To address quality and strive to improve outcomes for children and families, the need for leadership models and innovative systems-building approaches has increased. Systems development efforts have placed greater demand on the need for more coordination and improved infrastructure. The fragmentation of the early childhood field across many different political and administrative authorities offers countless opportunities for collaboration. Multiple approaches, including QRIS and professional development systems, also lend themselves well to collaboration.

Across the country, communities have had access to different funding sources for systems-building efforts. These sources have focused on increasing infrastructure, aligning and linking programs, improving compensation, and delivering more efficient, effective, and seamless services to children and families. Some communities, cities, counties, and states have task forces, work groups, or advisory boards that formed with the sole purpose of developing comprehensive and integrated early learning systems.

Defining Systems

A system is an organized way in which regularly interacting or independent entities come together to create a more unified whole. Through collaboration, organizations are better able to fulfill a common purpose or organize ideas, functions, or procedures. In the ECE field, systems help coordinate multiple services, programs, and funding streams to meet the needs of young children and their families.

Helene Stebbins (2012), deputy director at Alliance for Early Success, suggests that early childhood systems have two components: direct services and infrastructure support. Direct services are the programs that work with children and families, including child care programs such as family child care, center-based care, Head Start, and state preschools. Direct services may also include early intervention, nutrition and health, and family support programs. Infrastructure support includes all the pieces that make it possible to provide direct services—program standards, funding structures, regulations and policies, and professional development or workforce supports.

Systems-building efforts for ECE focus on improving or increasing programs and services for children and families. Authors Sharon Lynn Kagan and Kristie Kauerz (2012, 88) define an ECE system as "an orderly and comprehensive assemblage of interrelated elements that creates equitable, accessible, comprehensive, and quality services for young children." The BUILD Initiative, which works with early childhood leaders in states and at the national level to develop early childhood systems, defines systems as the programs, services, and policies that are connected or developed to help the young children in that state succeed.

Kagan, Kauerz, and the BUILD Initiative all approach systems that affect outcomes for children with a broad, multifaceted lens. In order to provide a positive outcome for a child, systems must increase opportunities for the whole family to thrive. This involves improving or integrating services or programs that support family financial stability, safety, health and mental health, and child care and early learning. Systems efforts must support each of these intersecting needs in order to support children's optimal development. Supporting systems efforts will require engaging stakeholders and ensuring accountability. It will also require coordinated leadership, finance strategies, and improved and aligned standards.

When writing about the BUILD Initiative work of 2007, Julia Coffman (2012, 201) describes how systems building may involve work in these areas:

- **Context**—Improving the political environment that surrounds systems so it produces the policy and funding changes needed to create and sustain systems
- **Components**—Establishing **high-performance programs and services** within systems that produce results for children and families
- **Connections**—Creating strong and effective **linkages** within and between systems that further improve results for children and families
- **Infrastructure**—Developing the **supports** that systems need to function effectively and with quality
- **Scale**—Ensuring that **comprehensive systems** are available to as many people as possible so they produce broad and inclusive results for children and families

Current ECE Systems Work

Today child care enables most parents in the United States to remain in the workforce. For example, 67 percent of children ages zero to twelve in the United States have parents in the labor force (California Child Care Resource & Referral Network 2015). Yet in California, one of the most populous states in the nation, child care spaces are available for only 25 percent of the state's children (Kidsdata.org 2017). Additionally, almost a quarter (23 percent) of children ages zero to five nationwide are living in poverty (California Child Care Resource & Referral Network 2015). Child care is critical to enabling parents to work and lift their families out of poverty.

There is now an unprecedented understanding and support for the need for high-quality early learning. Neuroscience research confirms that a child's early years are critical to healthy growth and development. High-quality early learning settings result in positive long-term outcomes.

Moreover, economists support the investment in ECE due to the long-term economic benefits to communities.

As a result, systems development efforts in the ECE field have increased as communities strive to improve or better align programs and services to deliver more efficient, effective, and seamless services to children and families. Many communities have task forces, work groups, or advisory boards comprised of multiple stakeholders that came together to develop comprehensive and integrated early learning systems. As Kagan and Kauerz (2012, 5) note, "This is an unprecedented time for thinking comprehensively about the needs of young children."

Systems-building efforts include initiatives aimed at addressing issues that affect children and families, such as homelessness, school-readiness, literacy, child care supply and equitable child care access, early intervention, and health-related challenges such as obesity reduction. Other system initiatives, such as professional development systems, QRIS, or workforce development systems, focus on improving ECE provisions or increasing child care quality. The goal is that with a more coordinated and systemic approach to these various issues, improved services can be delivered, resulting in improved outcomes for children, families, and communities.

The Complexities of Broad ECE Systems Work

ECE continues to be funded and supported through fragmented channels. Other than federally funded Head Start programs, funding for early childhood education mainly falls to the states through child care subsidy programs supported by federal Child Care and Development Block Grants (CCDBG) and Temporary Assistance for Needy Families (TANF) funds or through publicly funded preschool programs. Child care subsidy programs, as part of welfare reform, help low-income families find jobs and stay employed but don't necessarily support or promote the quality of the child care provided.

Early Head Start and other programs, such as transitional kindergarten, are expanding the type and supply of child care, yet the structure and policies may or may not increase or focus support on quality environments or teacher-child interactions. Many states have developed some quality improvement activities, such as professional development support or QRIS, which are specifically focused on improving the quality of child care. These investments vary widely in design and the degree to which they aim to increase quality of care or subsidize the costs for working parents.

In an address to Houghton Mifflin Harcourt's Conversations on Early Learning, Kagan (2015) stated, "Historically, in the US, we've started with programs and attempted to implement systems after the fact, in response to various needs. This means we don't have one coherent system when it comes to Early Childhood Education and this has created challenges." There are many different types of programs, each with its own set of guidelines, regulations, and funding sources. In addition, these vary from state to state, leading to confusion among parents and those in the ECE field. Most within the field have little understanding or ability to navigate these systems. The complexities also make it difficult to determine how to even approach making improvements.

Stacie Goffin and Valora Washington say that the essential question those in the field need to answer is: What defines early education as a field? To answer this question, Goffin and Washington (2007, 49–50) believe the ECE field must address two main challenges: "a performance gap, between articulation of high standards and uneven quality in practice, and a credibility gap, created by our reluctance to confront the field's self-protective conduct as it relates to our collective competence." The authors assert that the field has to wrestle with these gaps and answer some fundamental questions, including: Will the field determine competence as a collective entity and develop standards to hold those in the field accountable to one another? This step is essential for establishing a more coherent system, set of subfields, or subsystems.

To effectively build or align systems, organizations must step beyond the focus on a single program or service and look at the big picture. The end goal is an integrated and aligned holistic system that is greater than the sum of its parts. Achieving this requires focused attention on the infrastructure that supports all the separate and varied programs, including funding, policies, services, regulations, and more. To reimagine or redevelop infrastructure requires first understanding the interdependence on these various systems and programs and then determining ways to better align or integrate all parts from the ground up. It takes rebuilding the architecture from the foundation, which then lifts the whole system up in new and stronger ways.

Kagan (2015) identifies the following goals and subsystems she believes will strengthen this work:

- **Learning subsystem**—The standards, curriculum, workforce development, and family and community programs that impact learning environments. Improving these elements leads to the ultimate goal of higher quality care for children and families.
- **Provision subsystem**—Elements that impact the provision of care. Currently there are significant disparities in access to quality programs. When building and improving systems, organizations must work to ensure that all children are served in an equitable way.

- **Similar to Kagan's infrastructure subsystem**—The government entities, financial mechanisms, regulations and policies, and workforce development initiatives that support and sustain services.

Gretchen Ames (2015) developed a model as a way to demonstrate the current contexts of the ECE system. The outside box represents what Ames calls the Systems Level. Similar to Kagan's Infrastructure Subsystem, this level includes government, policy, and regulations. Ames notes that this level—especially funding and regulations—is complex and often split among several government branches. Many of the decisions affecting the early childhood education field are made at this level, sometimes without input from those operating within the other levels.

The Early Childhood Professionals box in Ames's model points out the hierarchical approach of the system. Those who work directly with children and families and are affected most by the design, funding, and decisions made at other levels receive the lowest compensation and have fewer opportunities for input. To change the system and strive toward greater equity, efficiency, effectiveness, and improved quality and outcomes for children and families, new leaders with innovative ideas are necessary.

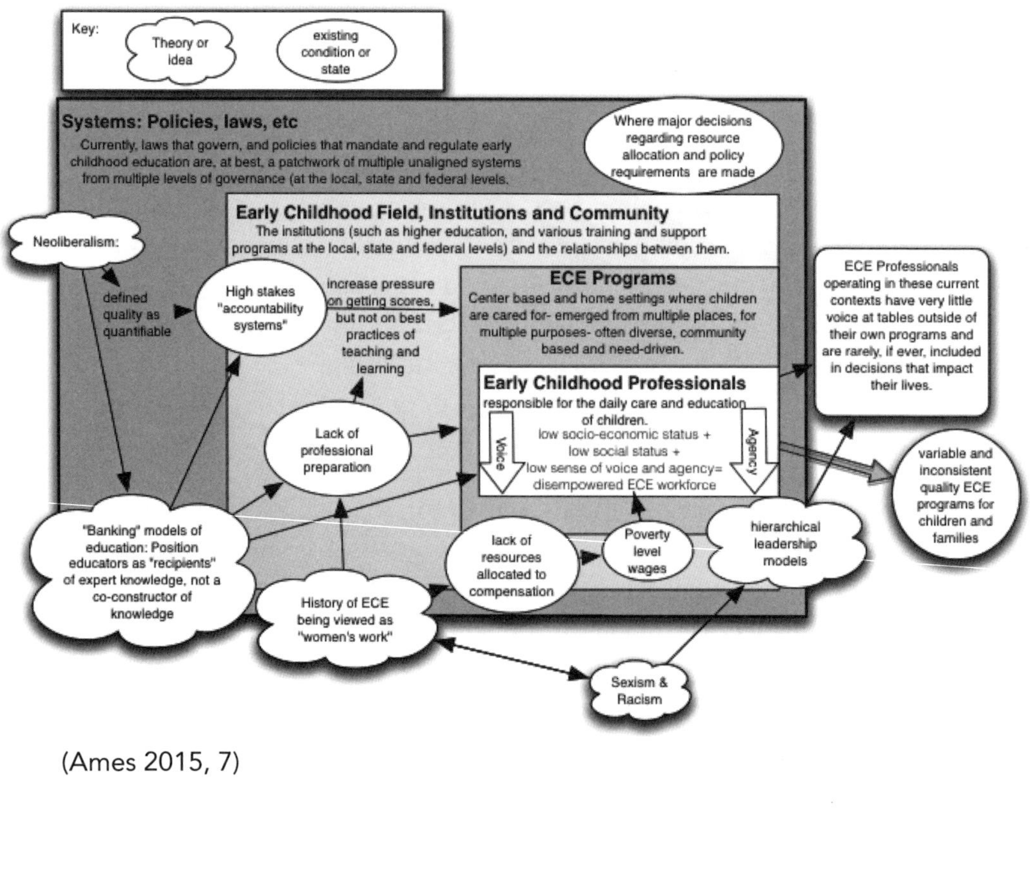

(Ames 2015, 7)

I also believe that building communities and systems in which children and families can thrive involves rethinking how the ECE field connects and aligns with other programs and systems. We know health, mental health, nutrition, adequate housing, and other needs are critical to a child's optimal development. Our field needs to be effective, strong, and sustainable to successfully strengthen and integrate all systems serving children and families.

Quality leadership at all levels is critical to the work of building successful systems. Classroom teachers, program administrators, parents, and community members are all an important part of building the political will and championing the work. To achieve common goals, it's imperative to have leaders who work in both direct services and in the infrastructure subsystems and can coordinate efforts to transform a collection of programs into an efficient and effective system.

Leadership models and skills are vital to initiate, champion, and sustain these efforts. Dean Clifford (2012, 164) asserts that effective leadership is critical for implementing early childhood systems work: "The collaboration involved in building an early childhood system requires sophisticated skills . . . even with limited funding, those local organizations with skilled leadership flourish, continually expanding and deepening their impact."

What Is Leadership?

We've all known leaders. People in all types of positions and in all kinds of organizations may have leadership strengths. But if we think back on the leaders we've known, it wasn't about the person's position or title or status. Leadership is more than that. And while leadership is partly about skills or capabilities, it's more than that as well. Leadership is an individual's ability to work with, inspire, and mobilize others to accomplish goals or achieve agreed-upon results.

According to Jane E. Dutton and Gretchen M. Spreitzer (2014), leadership is a kind of optimistic perspective. Leaders have the ability to see possibilities and bring out the best in people, as well as have the awareness that small actions can have a big impact. These leaders don't settle for mediocre and know that excellence can be expanded if one believes in and leads toward the extraordinary. Dutton and Spreitzer believe that quality leaders do not require formal power but instead have the ability to foster positive relationships with the focus and vision to be aspirational.

Leadership is also an active and dynamic state. It is not only inspiring others but also taking action and working toward improvement. Goffin (2013, 57) reminds us that leadership "is an activity rather than a role" and that a great leader "embraces learning, adapting, creating, and responds to emerging possibilities." It's as if leadership is about forward motion, always moving toward growth, change, and new directions. Great leaders don't settle for the status quo but forge ahead toward what could be. Leadership can be transformational.

A genuine leader is not a searcher for consensus but a molder of consensus.
—Martin Luther King Jr.

Finally, leadership is also about both action and knowledge. Some leaders inspire motivation and action for tasks. Other leaders possess great content knowledge to inform the task at hand. And although some leaders may have more innate leadership qualities or abilities, leadership skills and knowledge can be learned. Leadership skills are also strengthened and fine-tuned over time and with experience and reflection.

Qualities of Effective Leaders

All of us have a core set of values and personal qualities. Being aware of your values and the ways in which those values influence how you work and interact with others is crucial. To be an effective leader, one needs to be able to look inward and forward to identify values and develop or strengthen the leadership qualities needed to move his or her work and the field in the right direction. Maurice Sykes (2014, 11) believes that "anyone who wants to be a leader in the field of early childhood education must first make a personal commitment to doing the right thing for children and, even beyond that, must be guided by a set of leadership qualities."

Vision

Great leaders have vision. They have the ability to see through information overload to the heart of the issue. They shine a light on critical points and can focus attention on the truths that will inspire change and move the work forward. Effective leaders are forward looking and can idealize other possibilities. They are aspirational in their desire to work toward long-term goals and solutions. But more than that, they create hope and inspire others to work toward a vision. They help identify or establish a group's shared purpose or goal and demonstrate passion for the greater purpose. Leaders are agents of change and uphold a belief in transformation. This hope generated and modeled by leaders who imagine a better way through change explains why people will often rally around leaders.

Integrity

Integrity is critical to quality leadership while building systems. For systems-building work to truly occur, leaders must always hold out the potential of what could be above all individual and organizational self-interests. Integrity is about knowing the greater goal is more important than self-interests and acknowledging that others may have the best ideas. A leader with integrity continually strives toward the loftier goal beyond her or his own ideas or self-interests. Ultimately, integrity is about doing the right thing even when no one is looking. It is about always staying true to what is right even when things get difficult.

Integrity is not only about upholding strong moral principles, decency, and fairness; it's also about maintaining wholeness. It is about cohesion, togetherness, and solidarity. Integrity enables leaders to remain true to the higher cause of the work while effectively bringing together all system components and programs. Integrity is about being selfless but also self-confident.

Respect

A significant aspect of leadership is the ability to build and maintain high-quality connections and relationships. This begins with the skills and commitment to respectfully work with others. Respect must be deep, honest, and meaningful. Great leaders honor and see value in all those with whom they work and appreciate and include each person's abilities, achievements, and ideas.

To be respectful, one must truly listen to others and seek to understand them without judgment. Positive leaders expect and assume that each person is bringing her or his best self and ideas to the process. This allows leaders to show it is possible to respect all ideas and welcome all viewpoints. One can disagree with the ideas or viewpoints. But to be truly respectful, one may have an opinion on or judge the ideas but not the person. Part of leadership is to create an environment and process where all ideas are welcome. This allows the free flow of ideas in a respectful dialogue, keeping the process moving toward shared goals.

Trust

For all involved to have faith in the leadership and the process, there must be trust. Ultimately, systems work is about relationships—people working together toward a common vision. And as Linda Lambert (2002, 57) and colleagues state, "Honesty and trust are fundamental to relationships." A leader sets the tone by helping to establish an honest and open process. Building on the respect afforded each person, a leader develops trust by respectfully engaging others and welcoming all viewpoints and ideas. People will participate if they trust they will be heard and that their opinions matter. This trust has to be actively lived, demonstrated, and pursued. Leaders must model it and be ever watchful and mindful about creating open, honest, and trusting environments and conversations.

Openness

To be a respectful leader and build trust, one must be open to different people, viewpoints, and ideas. A leader is also open to learning and understands and is comfortable with change and transitions. Leadership is about possibilities, and that requires embracing change and being open to the idea that things will be different tomorrow than they are today. Leaders also must be open to new information and understand there is much they don't know. Sykes (2014, 9) states, "To really be a leader, you need to understand that you always have more to learn." He adds, "To be a good person, and indeed to be a great leader, you need to be humble yourself. But more than that, you need to look beneath the surface of other people. People are complex, and their lives are complex. And if you jump to hasty conclusions about them, you're missing opportunities" (27). Remaining open as a leader creates space for new opportunities.

Knowledge, Curiosity, and Reflection

When coming into a leadership role, it is key to have knowledge, but more importantly, one must have an ongoing desire and commitment to continue learning. Knowledge is not passive. There is always more to know, and there are always others who know things you don't. Effective leaders have an ongoing desire to remain curious and always seek out additional knowledge and information.

Passionate curiosity is essential to leadership knowledge and quality. Leaders read, research, listen, and strive to understand. As Sykes (2014, 36) notes, "A knowledgeable leader is not someone who is all knowing. Rather he or she is someone who is all seeking." He adds, "To be an authentic leader, you need to be curious and to take calculated risks about the things you don't yet know" (48). Leaders who are curious ask questions and are eager to take on tough issues. As Holly Elissa Bruno (2012, 5) explains, "The mental agility fostered by boundless curiosity allows a leader to take risks and envision alternatives, even when the proven approach still works."

Effective leaders must also be reflective. They must be able to reflect on what they know, what has happened, what they have done, and what they could do. They have to analyze and learn from prior experiences and prior knowledge to be able to look ahead. Without reflection, leadership can become stuck and remain static, unable to transform and move forward in new and more effective ways. A successful leader also knows that knowledge is a tool. Knowledge growth and development, therefore, must include reflection and increased learning in different knowledge areas:

- **Self-knowledge**—An understanding and awareness of one's values, strengths, and motivations is important. Self-knowledge is a foundational piece from which to build on, to understand who you are. What are you good at? What difference are you trying to make in the world? What do you believe in? Without knowing oneself, it will be difficult to know where one is going, how to get there, and how to lead others. With self-knowledge, a leader can use personal strengths to address challenges and foster self-knowledge in others.

Leadership and learning are indispensable to each other.
—John F. Kennedy

- **Knowledge of others**—Having knowledge of those who are in this work with you is also important. Knowing about the interests, passions, strengths, and challenges of others helps inform your leadership approach. Understanding the knowledge and strengths of those involved in order to identify team members who could benefit from more information, additional perspectives, or resources is helpful as well.
- **Content knowledge**—Having knowledge in the subject area in which they propose to lead is critical for leaders. Leaders need some level of information and experience about the subject and content of the

work. This includes the ability to translate the knowledge into action and ideas so people "know what you are talking about and that your knowledge base comes from a rich body of experience, research, and practice" (Sykes 2014, 41). Effective leaders also know and understand the different sides of an issue. They must develop a global perspective, including opposing viewpoints, to truly understand the content.

- **Leadership knowledge**—Through the leadership journey, leaders must continue to grow, increasing their repertoire and tool kit of leadership knowledge and skills. Through reading, reflection, experience, and interactions with mentors and others, leaders can continually grow their knowledge base of effective leadership.

Purpose and Initiative

Leaders have a strong sense of purpose. They are motivated and driven to work toward goals and attain end results. They also strive to reach their full potential with purpose and meaning. This can inspire and encourage others to also have purpose. A colleague of mine once said in a meeting that she sees her own sense of purpose as one of her greatest strengths. She added that she is effective because she knows where she is going. As a leader in her organization and in her work, she is headed forward with purpose and direction.

Leaders get things done. They have an internal drive to make things better and move toward a better outcome. Leaders both inspire action and take action to work toward change. They will take on a challenge, even if risky or difficult. Rather than wait for others or see how it might go, leaders jump in, take action, and lead the way. Leaders take the initiative to challenge the status quo and not settle for how things currently are. Leaders don't accept the things they cannot change—they strive to change the things they cannot accept.

Dependability, Perseverance, and Flexibility

For people to have trust in leadership, they need to know that the leaders are dependable. Leaders provide stability and can be counted on when the road is unclear or difficult. Leaders have a strong work ethic and will remain reliable and steadfast through conflict, problem solving, or long, complex tasks and initiatives. Without dependability, it will be challenging to make any progress with systems-building efforts.

To remain dependable, leaders must persevere even when times get tough. They need to have a stick-to-it attitude and a collaborative can-do approach. This perseverance encourages those involved with systems-building efforts to continue to pursue a collaborative solution. They know it can be done and are able to inspire those around them to stay strong and keep at it. Systems-building work can be long and arduous. It can involve building and maintaining many different relationships, working through several tasks, and dealing with multiple agencies, personalities, funding issues, and more. To remain dedicated to the vision and continuously see the work through to the end goal requires perseverance.

Leaders also have to be flexible. Change is inevitable, and things do not always go as planned. Effective leaders have to be comfortable with ambiguity and be able to persevere in times of uncertainty and change. Leaders must adapt, sometimes quickly, to new information or unseen changes. Leadership requires one to remain adaptable in order to take action and keep navigating toward progress.

Sense of Humor

Having a sense of humor is sometimes key to striving forward when something new or unforeseen happens. Humor allows a leader to see the fun in a situation and stay optimistic about the way forward. These actions also help others maintain momentum, even when things go differently than expected. A leader with a sense of humor keeps the mood positive and helps everyone work through possible alternatives. The ability to laugh also connects people and keeps them engaged. Humor can be a shared experience that unites the group and energizes team members for the task ahead.

Confidence

Leaders gain confidence over time as they face adversity and overcome challenges. Confident leaders have faced failure but have developed the ability, courage, and knowledge to get back up, figure out what to do, and keep at it. Leaders don't run from adversity; they stay calm and move into it, facing the challenge and acting on it. This leadership confidence is not cockiness but ability.

Inclusivity

Systems-building work requires a lot of knowledge and input across agencies and sectors. Therefore, it is critical that leaders bring together those who will inform and strengthen the work and include the necessary stakeholders. According to Tom Rath and Barry Conchie (2008, 21), "Effective leaders surround themselves with the right people and build on each person's strengths." This helps create ongoing buy-in on the work and also ensures that there are many different ideas, viewpoints, skills, and strengths on which to build a strong base. As Sykes (2014, 30) writes, "Great leaders are always on the lookout for people with diverse skills and perspectives who will be able to contribute to their leadership agenda."

To be truly inclusive requires humility. A genuinely inclusive leader honestly believes that she or he is no better than anyone else and recognizes the value in others. Humble and inclusive leaders encourage everyone to feel appreciated and valued. This fosters dedication to working together toward success. You can't fake this, because others will remember how you made them feel and whether each person's contributions were valued. Every single person adds value and has strengths and ideas to contribute.

Over the years I have observed that some attributes of leadership are universal and are often about finding ways of encouraging people to combine their efforts, their talents, their insights, their enthusiasm and their inspiration to work together.
—Queen Elizabeth II

Roles of Effective Leaders

Leaders play a variety of roles. Sometimes they lead the way. At other times leaders serve more as coaches or mentors, motivating and inspiring others to lead. Leaders often voice, create, and facilitate opportunities to work for change. But leaders, in their varied roles, always have an eye on the future and the desire to transform in a new way. To build systems, leaders need to work with others toward an agreed-upon direction and agreed-upon goals. The following leadership roles are effective to work toward system-level change.

Nothing will work unless you do.
—Maya Angelou

Inspire and Build Shared Vision

Leaders define the vision and set the tone for the work ahead. Effective leaders are passionate about what they hope to accomplish, and they champion those aspirations. They work with others to identify shared goals and build consensus and motivation to endeavor toward those goals. They know that when people are truly involved in developing a shared vision, they feel a strong commitment to a common purpose.

Model the Way

Effective leaders, through their words and actions, demonstrate what is possible. They are consistent and clear in their values and model the way by staying true to the vision. They maintain efforts to forge ahead and continue to see the opportunities and hold out the potential of a new way. People look to leaders as role models, so it is important for leaders to make sure their actions match their values and goals. They must model what they hope for and expect in others.

A sign of a good leader is not how many followers you have, but how many leaders you create. —Mahatma Gandhi

Empower Others

Strong leaders foster collaboration and teamwork. They encourage others to participate by sharing power and responsibility, and they know that those closest to a situation often have the best opportunities and expertise to make choices and take action. Leaders enable and embolden others to take on tasks and work to reduce barriers for all to succeed. Leaders know that success encourages continued success. They realize the importance of supporting and celebrating the ongoing accomplishments of others. Leaders keep everyone motivated to stay on task and continue to strive toward the collective vision.

Facilitate Others' Best Work

All participants have something to contribute. An effective leader helps set the tone and provides opportunities for all to have a voice and for all ideas to be valued. This includes facilitating a process for all to feel comfortable and ready to bring their best efforts forward. In a highly functioning collaborative team, all members are able to grow in their own leadership capabilities and increase their knowledge and skills. Facilitating others' best work means holding high standards while welcoming all to join in and lift up the entire team and effort. With effective leadership, each member of the collaborative team is viewed as a leader and expert.

Challenge the Process

Joyce Kaser and colleagues (2006, 5) state that effective leaders both "question and work to change the status quo." To effectively work toward systems change requires leaders to examine how things have been done and strive to envision new ways of achieving goals. Things won't change without taking the risk to challenge current realities and endeavor to improve upon them.

To challenge the process requires leaders to continually question the current status of things. In his remarks at the 2016 Harvard Graduate School of Education commencement, James Ryan, who was dean of the school at the time, stated the importance of asking the following questions:

- **"Wait, what?"** Because it is necessary to slow down, get clarification, and question what is happening. Asking, "Wait, what?" prevents us from making assumptions and challenges us to assess why things are the way they are.
- **"I wonder why . . . ?/I wonder if . . . ?"** Because if we ask why, we remain curious and continue to question why things are the way they are. And if we ask, "I wonder if," then we are thinking about how we can improve things (Harvard Education 2016).

With each of these questions, we challenge what is and begin the work of thinking about and creating what could be.

Champion Social Justice

Good leaders strive to mitigate social and economic inequities and uphold social justice for all children and families. They work to bring voice to social justice issues and endeavor to create high-quality programs and design systems that lift all children up, especially those from underresourced communities, so that all have equitable opportunities.

This work includes looking at the structure and model of leadership. If leadership is seen as hierarchical, with only some having power, then the model begins to systemically build in inequities. Leaders must be intentional and vigilant in creating a system where all have value and all have a voice to give input and contribute. A leader's role is to champion equity and authentically work to include and stand up for all involved.

Addressing System Inequities

As leaders, it is our responsibility to uphold a commitment to social justice. At a system level, leaders can work to ensure that strong programs and organizations are in place to promote social justice and that all practices strive to level the playing field and not perpetuate system inequities. To do this, we must first take a hard look and be honest about any possible inequities. Sykes (2014, 58) suggests that leaders need to have a "working knowledge of the social and political context of their environment and a strategic plan to apply the knowledge of the injustice they are trying to address, and they are able to exercise the required level of political acumen necessary to remedy the situation."

As women, we must stand up for ourselves. . . . We must stand up for each other. . . . We must stand up for justice for all.
—Michelle Obama

Acknowledge Assumptions, Power, and Diverse Interests

To truly champion social justice and inclusion in systems-building work requires opportunities and processes in which participants can both acknowledge and be transparent about their own assumptions, any felt or perceived power imbalances, and different interests. To address these potential pitfalls, leaders must ask themselves and others many difficult questions:

- Where is there power and privilege?
- Where are there inequities?
- What can be done to expand equity and social justice?
- Who isn't currently included in the process but should be? Why are some not included?
- Can we name and understand the power dynamics that are part of our system and decision-making practices?
- What strategies would make this a more equitable process or learning community for all?

These questions and others will help leaders to begin the process of acknowledging and understanding where there are underlying assumptions, inequities, and/or power imbalances that hinder a truly inclusive social justice approach.

Leadership Competencies

Knowledge is the sum of what one knows or understands and the facts or information acquired through experience or education. Competence, however, is about what one does with knowledge and understanding. One exhibits competence by putting knowledge into actionable behavior. Effective leaders make things happen and influence transformational change.

Personal Competence

Personal competence is the knowledge, experience, and skill that one brings to the leadership role. To be personally competent, one must cultivate an ever-growing body of knowledge but also be able to apply, adapt, and use that knowledge in different situations. This includes assuming responsibility for understanding what you know, acknowledging what you don't know, and gathering more information when needed. According to Sykes (2014, 73), competence at the personal level requires "continual participation in the learning process and the active application of new knowledge in one's day-to-day life."

Personal competence is the ability to operate at one's best with the humility and understanding that there is always more to learn. Leaders strive to be increasingly proficient and capable and seek ways to take their knowledge and skills to the next level.

Organizational and Political Competence

Being an effective leader for systems change requires organizational and political competence. A competent leader at the organizational level understands how organizations work, including the complexities and layers of power and influence. He or she knows that policy is developed and implemented at the organizational level and understands how policy can shape organizational and systems work. A competent leader also has the ability to analyze organization and system policies and strategies and determine where changes or improvements could be made.

CHAPTER 2

Discovering Your Leadership Style

THINK ABOUT the leaders you have known. What kind of leader do you want to be? What kind of leaders have you worked with in the past? Do you aspire to be like them, or do you hope to do things very differently? Consider your own values, style, skills, knowledge, and the approach you plan to bring to your leadership work. Learning about leadership models and ideas as you begin to craft your own leadership style is also important.

The first step to understanding leadership styles and models is to think about how leadership influences the work. Identify the sources of power and who has the authority to make decisions.

Leadership Authority—Sources of Power

Leadership is not always about attaining a particular position within an organization. Ask any five leaders how they rose to a leadership position, and you may get five very different answers. Often leaders came to leadership roles through different journeys and for different reasons. But leadership does include some level or assumption of power or authority. This does not have to be hierarchical or even permanent but instead may be about the current situation or current roles. It is critical to acknowledge, understand, and support power structures developed and decided on as part of the systems-building process. Leadership authority generally arises through expertise, institutional power, and/or positional power:

- **Expertise**—Some come into a leadership role because of their knowledge of a particular situation or topic. Leaders may be summoned to join the work by those involved as the need for expertise arises. In other instances, the leader may come from within the group or organization and begin to assume a leadership role. Group members may look to one with expertise in the topic to lead the organization in shaping the goals or values of the group or to take on leadership of a specific task.

- **Institutional power**—Sometimes leadership authority comes from the power granted by the institution or organization. If certain institutions are a significant partner, important contributor, or participant in the systems-building efforts, then individuals from this entity may need to assume leadership authority. For example, in any systems-building effort, there may be a lead agency or an entity that has more institutional power. Perhaps this is a government entity or the organization with the largest investment or most to gain. This may thrust that institution and the individuals representing it into a leadership role.
- **Positional power**—If one has a leadership position within an organization or the systems-building structure, then a leadership role in systems-building efforts may be an assumed role. For example, I serve on the leadership team of a large QRIS that comprises those with positional power—such as executive directors—within the partner organizations. Each of these executive directors is in a position of leadership at their own organization, but they come together to collaborate in a collective leadership role, forming a decision-making body. But so much about leadership is also relational and can occur at multiple levels within and across organizations and systems. So sometimes leadership is about the role one is willing to assume at any given time.

Leadership Models

There are different ways of being a leader and various approaches to leadership. Some leadership models and styles are more autocratic in that the leaders have more control over all decision-making responsibilities and the power structure is from the top down. Although this style may be effective in some organizations, sectors, or situations, I have focused on more collaborative, consultative, and participatory approaches that I believe are more effective for systems-building efforts. An autocratic leader makes decisions, sets policy, and generates all ideas. But for effective systems change, new ideas, creativity, and innovation are key. To effectively work across systems or sectors requires a collective or shared approach that includes all who are involved and affected. Honest work for change requires dynamic input and ideas from everyone. No one person has all the answers. The work is successful because it is done together.

Values-Based Leadership

Values-based leadership is the ability and desire to focus on what matters most and make decisions that are aligned with these values. It is actually easier to make choices and navigate through challenging situations when you have clearly defined your values. Values guide one's decisions, actions, and choices no matter what the position or situation, enabling one to remain calm and confident.

The career of Harry M. Jansen Kraemer Jr. is a good example of values shaping one's future path. Kraemer, the former CEO of a multibillion-dollar health care company, became a professor at Northwestern University's Kellogg School of Management and often invites CEOs of companies to be guest lecturers in his classes. He notes that students frequently ask the guest at what point in their career they decided to become a CEO. Most of the CEOs reply that they never thought they would be a CEO and never planned on it. Instead, they were focused on doing a good job and making a positive impact, and this work led to their promotions. Kraemer himself states that his goal has always been to make a difference. His priority is to always learn and grow and add value to the organization he is a part of. When Kraemer began working for the health care company, he had a small cubicle office. He never knew or cared if he would be promoted, but instead focused on the values he held dear and his outlook on life. He wanted to do good work, value others, be respectful, and make a difference. Throughout his career, Kraemer remained focused on doing the right thing and putting the goals and needs of his team and his organization above his own. The company recognized Kraemer for his values and eventually made him CEO for his work (Kraemer 2011).

Being a values-based leader means knowing who you are and what you stand for. To embrace a values-based leadership approach, begin by taking a thorough inventory of your strengths, core values, and beliefs. Do you have a vision for your leadership work? Do you have a strong sense of purpose? Do you have the knowledge you will need? Do you feel confident in your leadership role and ready to take initiative?

Remaining aligned with your values requires continuous self-reflection and awareness. It is only through this level of thought and evaluation that a values-based leader can grow, learn, and incorporate lessons learned. A values-based leader must also have the self-confidence to stand firm and calm in the face of adversity and remain true to those values. Self-confidence also ensures a leader will make decisions from a values-based perspective. Lastly, a values-based leader must have the humility to never forget where he or she came from. The importance of those remaining aligned with one's own core values will continually inspire a leader to stay true to what matters most.

Leading with Heart

To lead with heart is to care about and genuinely appreciate and value the contributions of others in the organization. Strong leaders know that positive attention and recognition are powerful motivators. To this end, they work to build a collaborative climate made up of productive teams. A leader sets the tone by showing appreciation for everyone's contributions and creating a culture of caring. Jim Kouzes and Barry Posner (2012) provide ideas on how leaders can encourage working from the heart:

- **Recognize contributions.** Noticing what people contribute to the efforts helps people feel good about their work. Even small gestures let people know their strengths and contributions are valued.
- **Expect the best.** Believing in others is a powerful motivator. When you expect the best and recognize people's strengths, then all involved endeavor to reach the established goals. If you expect people to succeed, they often will, especially if they have been given support along the way.
- **Be clear about goals.** Providing clear information on goals and the process helps people succeed. Feeling good and striving to give your all is hard when you don't fully understand your role. Leaders need to be honest and transparent, and to set a clear direction. When leaders establish definitive goals, they set a caring tone and provide team members with opportunities to strive toward what matters.
- **Give regular feedback.** Throughout the process, let people know what is going well. Checking in regularly provides opportunities to recognize accomplishments and acknowledge any challenges or areas that need support or assistance. This allows people to learn, problem solve, and address any confusion or uncertainty. Through regular feedback, people know their ideas and challenges matter. They also understand that someone cares and will provide the input necessary to encourage everyone to succeed.

Nancy Rosenow defines heart-centered leadership as knowing and accepting oneself so well as to fearlessly lead from a place of kindness and love. She suggests that heart-centered leaders are at peace with themselves, and as a result they can be genuinely honest without feeling threatened. They can lead with kindness because they know and embrace their own strengths and understand themselves in a way that is free of negative judgment. This helps leaders see the strengths in others, focus on the positive, and choose love over fear.

Rosenow says heart-centered leaders value kindness and courage. They believe in celebrating others and celebrating often. They celebrate the small things and appreciate effort and dedication. By celebrating even the smallest accomplishments, an organization, team, or system can become more supportive, positive, and joyful. As a result, people feel valued and free to be authentic. And when team members remain true to themselves, they are committed to the values and mission of the work: "Work is done with a sense of purpose and dedication to something that transcends each individual. The satisfying feeling of contributing to the greater good flourishes" (Rosenow 2016, 19).

Leadership for Social Justice

As leaders, it is our responsibility to make sure we are building systems that elevate all children and families. We must be clear and focused on ensuring that all components of the system, including the organizations and communities, help all children strive toward their full potential. To be a leader in the field of ECE is to be an agent of change who endeavors to make things better. A transformational leader stands up for what is right and just.

We also do this because we know that education can be the great equalizer. A high-quality early childhood system has the potential to alter social and economic circumstances and eliminate barriers. Strong and just systems can bring about change in communities and societies and help improve outcomes for children and families. Many children in this country get off to an uneven start due to the social, political, and economic constructs of society and the systems in place. As effective leaders, our task is to ensure that ECE systems lift up children and families.

This is not always easy. Bruno (2013, 23) explains, "Leadership is the courage to do the right thing regardless of pressure to take the easy path." Doing or saying nothing sometimes feels easier. But leaders push themselves to take action when injustice occurs. They champion what is right and are willing to work to make an impact and ensure a level playing field.

For you as a leader, this requires a deep awareness of yourself and your core values. We leaders must be aware of our own personal moral compass and values and decide where we stand. We must ask ourselves, Is this what I would want for myself or my child? What do I feel is right and wrong? What is fair and unfair? Each leader must decide this for herself or himself. Only with this knowledge are leaders able to develop a strong conviction and sense of social justice at an individual level. What we build must work well for everyone's children. If we remain vigilant on the point of equity, then we are standing for social justice.

In establishing your own sense of social justice, check your assumptions, especially about power and privilege. We know what we know because of our experiences. We have to be willing and committed to step into what we don't know and understand things from different perspectives. We have all developed biases and made assumptions, sometimes unknowingly because of the social, political, and economic contexts in which we have lived. Stepping away from these biases and assumptions to expand or change our knowledge and viewpoints requires dedication and hard work, listening, reflection, and humility. As Sykes (2014, 64) puts it, "You must identify the fibers of your own moral fabric in no uncertain terms." Then you can understand deeply who you are at your core and act from strong moral ground and from your heart.

Leadership and Equity

In Alameda County in California's Bay Area, the Emerging Leaders Fellowship is offering a unique approach to developing leadership to address racial equity. Offered through the Alameda County Office of Education in coordination with the Alameda County Early Care and Education Planning Council, the Emerging Leaders Fellowship is working to prepare the next generation of leaders to better serve diverse communities. Noticing that the diversity of those working in leadership roles in ECE did not reflect the diversity of the children in the county, Neva Bandelow, a national fellow in the Equity Leaders Action Network, began the project as a way to influence children and families in her own community. The eighteen-month program began in August 2016 and includes cofacilitator Dr. LaWanda Wesley, guest speakers, consultants, and mentors who guide participants through the initial two-day orientation and the seventeen monthly sessions that follow. Participants attend the monthly sessions, where they read related materials, set individual goals to create their own projects, and share and learn from each other in a community of practice format. The program topics focus on systemic racial and social injustice with an emphasis on early learning impact (Alameda County 2016):

- envisioning the future as an ECE leader
- the evolution of transformational leadership
- defining equity, social justice, and leadership

Fellows look at historical, national, and local systems; identify current inequities and gaps; and make plans to address those inequities and gaps. The program includes embedded mentors to support the emerging leaders with their projects and to help with skill building. In addition, the program contains a succession-planning component in which mentors and participants think together about best practices for sustaining ongoing leadership for racial equity. The Emerging Leaders Fellowship is made possible through professional development funds and participant fees.

The Importance of Relationships

At its core, leadership is a relationship. Leadership is never about doing something or accomplishing things alone. Others are always involved. Leaders work with and inspire others. It is the quality of the relationships that matters most. These relationships, if positive, can lead to extraordinary results. When a leader is able to foster relationships grounded in respect, trust, honesty, and confidence within an organization, great things can be accomplished. So much of what we are able to achieve is about who we know. Many leaders will tell you that the best way to be effective is to build positive relationships.

Building and fostering positive relationships takes time and effort. Often I don't know at the time if the person I'm meeting will be someone I may collaborate with in the future. So I'm mindful to always be friendly, positive, and respectful with everyone I meet. I also think it's important to be genuine with people. I always try to just be myself. I let my passions, vision, leadership qualities, and interests shine through. I make a point to get to know people and learn about the work they do and what their interests and passions are as well. Finding connections with those you meet and taking note of the similar goals, activities, or target populations of your work is beneficial.

Maintaining these relationships over time is also worthwhile. Effective leaders take the time to build a robust network of connections. Stay in touch with people, and keep informed on their work and achievements. One thing I do is forward articles, stories, events, or opportunities that I think someone may be interested in. This keeps us connected and demonstrates that I know about their interests and will take the time to share information and ideas. Years later an opportunity to collaborate may arise when someone's knowledge, expertise, perspective, skills, or experiences may be valuable to the work ahead.

To better understand leadership as a relationship, Kouzes and Posner (2012) looked into the personal qualities and traits that people admire in leaders. Consistently over time, people responded with the same four characteristics: honest, forward-looking, competent, and inspiring. They concluded that credibility was key to quality leadership and to building strong relationships with leaders. Above all, people must believe in and feel they can trust leaders. Leaders must have vision and a competent level of expertise or knowledge in the topic at hand. But people also want to feel inspired by leaders. This again speaks to the point that leadership is a relationship; leaders must be credible and inspiring to those engaged in the work.

Kaser and colleagues learned from their Leadership Academy that leaders find great value in networking and relationships. They help leaders to learn from others and to share problems and strategies. Kaser (2006, 27) and her colleagues state, "Change in organizations is so complex that it cannot occur without strong relationships among people making up a variety of networks, some that exist within the boundaries of an organization and some that go outside." To bring about change and achieve long-term goals, focusing on people and relationships and maintaining strong networks is critical.

I've learned that people will forget what you said, people will forget what you did, but people will never forget how you made them feel.
—Maya Angelou

Servant Leadership

Servant leaders are mindful about how their leadership serves others. They dedicate themselves to listening and helping those around them. Servant leaders are more concerned about others than their own self-promotion. These kinds of leaders strive to be of service to the greater good. They are very altruistic and driven to do the best they can by others. Many leaders in the ECE field are more committed to the work they do on behalf of children and families than they are to their own advancement. Servant leadership has a serene and peaceful element, as such leaders are most concerned with the purpose rather than the complexities, challenges, or conflicts that are part of their efforts.

Servant leaders can be effective at encouraging others to do their best work, as they are not inhibited by the idea of those around them succeeding or taking on leadership roles. These leaders welcome a collective effort to tackle the problems and work together toward the larger goals. Servant leaders inspire up-and-coming leaders to think deeply about their own values and purpose, encouraging all to stay focused on the vision and communities they serve.

Constructivist Leadership

Constructivism is the theory that people construct meaning based on "their previous knowledge, beliefs, and experiences" (Lambert et al. 2002, 1). Both individuals and organizations bring past experiences, beliefs, values, and culture to the process of learning and constructing new knowledge. This influences how we interact with people, interpret and integrate new ideas, and build new knowledge.

For constructivist leaders, the emphasis is on learning and continuously constructing knowledge from a place of connectedness and community. Persons exist and learn in social ecological systems. They build knowledge because of relationships, interdependence, and diversity. These relationships and connections form the basis for all current and future possibilities.

Constructivist leadership "is about transformation of self, others, organizations, and society" (Lambert et al., xviii). Constructivist leaders recognize that learning and change occur through this interplay between people and communities. Therefore, these types of leaders find ways to build a trusting environment in which all can interact, share, reflect, and build knowledge together. They enable everyone to contribute and build on the diverse knowledge and skills of each group member.

Diversity and equity are essential to constructivist leadership. Diversity provides complexity and multiple perspectives and allows different viewpoints and possibilities to be considered. To construct new knowledge, different ideas to challenge our preconceived ways of thinking and old patterns of thought is essential. This requires equitable relationships that are built on mutual reciprocity and respect. If we do not view this information sharing and process as equal nor believe that all have something of value and significance to share, then the relationships for constructing knowledge together cannot be formed. A balance of power and purpose must exist to drive the learning process.

Leading productive conversations is at the heart of constructivist leadership. Through conversation, new knowledge and shared meaning are derived. Conversations are the method for the reciprocal sharing of viewpoints and working toward shared purpose and goals. Conversations can also inspire creativity and innovation. Leading such conversations, therefore, is key to ensuring they are deep and meaningful and include equitable sharing.

Adaptive Leadership

Adaptive leadership is about understanding the field's challenges and then figuring out how best to resolve them. At its heart, adaptive leadership is about change, but to determine the best ways to adapt, an adaptive leader must have a strong grasp of the issues at hand. So initially, adaptive leadership involves learning about the gaps, conflicts, unresolved problems, challenges, and systemic issues of the field. Adaptive leadership is then about striving toward a new way of making choices and resolving issues. It is also about changing the nature of one's work to better align behavior with values.

Goffin and Washington (2007, 49) believe that in the ECE field, primary adaptive issues are a "performance gap," involving inconsistent standards and uneven quality, and a "credibility gap" as the field struggles to confront and define competence. They suggest people in the field come together to learn and understand the "discrepancies between the field's espoused values and its actual behaviors" (50). The adaptive work then shifts to how best to use this new knowledge to resolve the issues, change behavior, and ultimately move the field forward.

According to Goffin and Washington, adaptive leaders don't have to be those in leadership positions; instead, these leaders are simply those who are ready to take action and work for change. The authors believe that adaptive leadership is like constructivist leadership in that diversity is critical to this work. Adaptive leaders need the ability to facilitate complex and challenging discussions, learn from different viewpoints, and inspire meaningful change. Emerging leaders must be ready for new levels of listening, learning, cooperation, teamwork, and communication among and between people from different perspectives.

Motivational Leadership

What drives us to do what we do? Why do we make the decisions we make? Motivation gives us direction and purpose and drives our actions, decisions, and choices. But how does motivation develop? "Everything we do is influenced by a complex system of human needs," state Lynn R. Marotz and Amy Lawson (2007, 30). We behave in different ways to try to satisfy these needs. These needs are biological but are also influenced by external factors such as culture, environment, and experiences. Therefore, motivation is unique to each individual. What drives each person to action varies, as does how we dedicate our time and energy.

Motivation can be basic in nature, such as the need for food, water, shelter, and safety. These basic needs are the most essential life-sustaining motivators. Needs may also be emotional or relational, such as the need for feeling as if we belong, the need for social connection, and the need for friendship. Other motivators may be a need to feel important, successful, or appreciated by others. But many of us also have a need to feel purposeful, to continue to learn and grow, to develop and use our talents to express ourselves creatively, or to tackle problems. This yearning to think, create, and figure things out is motivating.

At work these motivating factors may play out similarly. We want to feel physically comfortable and safe. We need to feel safe to try out new ideas, voice opinions, and strive to realize our goals and vision. This safety occurs in work environments with employers and coworkers who are supportive and both promote and encourage contributions and professional growth. We need to be appreciated in our work and want to be recognized for our accomplishments. People want to feel satisfied in their jobs and be given assignments and job responsibilities that are fulfilling and give them purpose and meaning. Employees also want to feel connected to their jobs and the people they work with and to have positive relationships with supervisors and colleagues.

Motivation also drives an individual's willingness to persist at a task or accomplish a goal. Knowing this can help determine how successful a leader will be or how the individuals in a group will strive toward a shared vision. A leader who understands what motivates team members and builds in challenges, opportunities, and recognition to meet those motivational needs will be more successful. Ultimately, systems-building efforts will succeed or fail depending on the leader's ability to motivate and influence the process. "Motivational leaders play a key role in assuring program success because they understand the 'big picture' and are not likely to get bogged down by small problems and minute detail. They must be able to assess situations efficiently, formulate responsive plans, and rally the resources necessary to achieve an objective" (Marotz and Lawson 2007, 55–56).

What does motivational leadership look like in practice? A motivational leader has the ability to connect with employees and colleagues by acknowledging them, their efforts, and their contributions. Such leaders bring out the best in people by noticing their work and making a point of doing things to recognize and build on successes and strengths. Recognition could be as simple as a kind word or a thoughtful card to acknowledge a success or recognize a well-handled challenge. It could also be acknowledging an individual's or team's accomplishments or good ideas during a meeting and encouraging others to share ideas and opinions. The acknowledgments do not need to be fancy or expensive; it is the thought that counts. One colleague I work with gives out theme-related treats, such as 100 Grand candy bars, to acknowledge great work.

Motivational leaders take the time to get to know people's interests, work styles, strengths, and limitations. By knowing the motivations and needs of team members, leaders can find ways to build on elements, welcome input and ideas, and encourage creativity. Encouragement can be given on an individual basis or to teams, either formally or informally. Some leaders might use a questionnaire or icebreaker activity to get to know more about people. Even just scheduling time together to brainstorm or share stories and ideas can help leaders and team members learn more about each other.

Motivational leaders also maintain positive and open lines of communication. Understanding that people want to feel safe and have trust in leadership and in the process, leaders make sure their communication style is transparent and honest. People will feel motivated to work toward goals if what is being communicated is genuine, trustworthy, and supportive. Allowing time to ask questions, have open dialogue, and freely acknowledge challenges, gaps in information, different ideas, and successes helps develop positive and respectful communication channels.

Providing a supportive and enjoyable environment is also the role of a motivational leader. It helps if people are comfortable, safe, and happy in their surroundings. This can increase morale, help people feel dedicated to the work, and develop a sense of pride in the workplace. One group I meet with regularly rotates meetings, having a different partner organization host the gathering each month. No matter who is hosting, the group makes sure the meeting room is set up with basic, yet fun, decorations. They may be something simple, like a few small plants or flowers, or brightly colored napkins or cups, but decorations help set a friendly tone and make people feel welcome and valued.

Motivational leaders support growth and development in others, encouraging the advancement of personal motivation among team members. Leaders promote setting personal goals and seeking new learning opportunities. They support those who take on new challenges and responsibilities and provide helpful feedback and encouragement. This genuine interest in and support of others builds commitment and dedication to improving knowledge and skills, reaching goals, and doing quality work. I've had times when this approach has led to a great staff member moving on to another job. That can be hard, but I always feel that I have done my job as a leader well when a team member is moving on to pursue further education opportunities or a different job as a result of the increased skills or knowledge gained while working with me.

Motivational Leaders . . .

- set a positive tone and establish an environment of respect, trust, and openness
- learn about others' strengths, challenges, values, and hopes
- encourage others to share ideas and opinions
- listen actively to others and remain open to diverse points of view and approaches
- communicate respectfully and openly
- recognize accomplishments and compliment others on their work
- strive to bring out the best in those around them
- support personal and professional growth and development in others

(Marotz and Lawson 2007)

Transformational Leadership

The goal of transformational leadership is to strive continuously toward a bigger vision. The primary focus is on creating change. This leadership style is effective for systems building as it is about transforming the way things are done or even redesigning an entire approach. The goal of transformational leadership is a paradigm shift or a new way of working. This type of leadership style builds on creativity and the ability to think outside the box or imagine new ways of doing things.

Transformation is change. It is transforming current ways of thinking and changing the way things are done. It may lead to changing "deeply held beliefs, knowledge, and habits of practice" (Kaser et al. 2006, 154). Transformative learning is more than just adding new knowledge—it is adding new ways of thinking, including shifts in assumptions and beliefs. Invoking this sort of change can be challenging and cause uncertainty. Adults going through transformative learning may have a tough time reacting in ways similar to children who go through a storming phase when learning new concepts. This can be a challenging time of frustration and irritability as one struggles with new learning and growth. Child development theorist Erik Erikson calls this phase disequilibrium.

Transformative learning is described in *Leading Every Day* as creating "cognitive dissonance, a disruption in someone's thinking, causing him or her to struggle to make sense of something that doesn't fit with their current ideas" (Kaser et al. 2006, 101). Here are things to consider during transformative learning:

- Adults will need time and support to resolve this dissonance by engaging with others and with facilitators who can provide guidance and mentoring.
- Providing dissonance-creating and dissonance-resolving activities that are relevant and meaningful to the participant is important.
- Opportunities to "develop new practices that are congruent with the new ideas they are constructing" need to be provided (101).
- Having support through a continuous cycle of "surfacing the new issues and problems . . . gaining new understandings from these experiences, translating new understandings from them, and recycling through the process" is essential (101).

Inspiration and motivation are key, as this approach requires stepping outside of what feels safe and familiar. Making a point of getting to know everyone and tapping into what matters to each person and what inspires each one in his or her work is critical. Equally important is building trust and a feeling of safety and confidence in the process. People need to know that their ideas, concerns, hopes, and fears are heard and valued.

Open communication and trust-building are important, as is establishing a shared decision-making process and forum for expressing ideas and views. Working together and ensuring that all have an equal voice is critical to the work. Keep in mind that people will accept and buy into that which they help create. Transformational leaders inspire and guide this change process.

Sometimes the process itself is transformational. Thinking through things together and equally sharing responsibility in the design and outcome may be new for people. It can also be hard work. For some, this is exciting and within their skill set or comfort zone. For others, this process may be very difficult or different than anything they've ever done. As a leader, it is necessary to be in tune with the members of the group and find ways to continue to motivate and inspire everyone.

It may be necessary to take small steps or move forward in tiny increments, depending on the nature of the work, the scale and scope of the transformative goals, and the strengths and skills of those involved. Taking small steps provides time for group members to adjust along the way while seeing the successes as they unfold. It will also allow opportunities for skill building, shared decision-making, and team-building exercises.

We cannot solve problems with the same thinking that created them.
—Albert Einstein

Leadership Skills: What Works in Early Childhood

Leadership in the ECE field, like many other fields, is primarily about one's ability to work with people. This is really at the heart of leadership. The leadership needed to help transform the early childhood field must also include the vision and skills to help address the complicated systems issues. Transforming the field will also require people working together toward shared goals; therefore, leaders will need the skills to foster relationships and collective action. And to nurture ongoing collaborative work, leaders will need the skills to help strengthen and build the capacity of collaborative partners and emerging leaders.

Individual Leadership Skills

Leadership is complex and requires a variety of skills to be successful and effective. If you are drawn to leadership or are already in a leadership role, chances are that you have many of the necessary skills. Most of the time, however, those who take on leadership roles have to learn a few skills as they go. Many new skills are developed along the way, and of course we are always learning more and improving and building on our existing skills.

In my experience, successful leaders in transformative systems building possess these abilities:

- think systemically
- develop and foster vision
- inspire and motivate others
- empower others
- challenge assumptions
- manage change
- build and sustain relationships
- cultivate transformation and learning
- build trust
- communicate respectfully
- take initiative
- exhibit risk taking
- demonstrate courage
- value continuous improvement
- persevere through challenges
- remain curious
- celebrate success

It's a big list, and leadership can seem like a monumental role. But one develops and expands on these skills over time and through experiences. Think about the skills you feel competent with and those that need further development. Keep in mind that skill development doesn't have to happen overnight; it will be ongoing work. One also may not need or use all these skills all the time. Leadership is about working with others who may have some of these skills already. Sometimes leadership skills are distributed between several individuals or members of a team.

Acts of Leadership

Sometimes it's easier to think of leadership as acts of leadership. Leadership need not be a constant, never-ending task, role, or burden. Sometimes leadership is a series of separate acts. There may be times when a particular task or role that is part of a larger initiative is a good match for your leadership skill set. Taking on such tasks and completing them or integrating them with other acts of leadership may be the most effective approach. But providing opportunities for others to take on leadership acts of their own to build their leadership skills is another option.

Valuing Others' Strengths

Growing and improving our own leadership skills is vital. Valuing the leadership strengths of others is also important. As we know, great leaders never work alone and are dedicated to those around them. Leaders notice and value strengths in others and find ways to nurture those leadership strengths. Truly effective leaders aren't only concerned about their own successes but are sure to help lift up and mentor other leaders around them.

Uncovering Others' Strengths

As Debra Ren-Etta Sullivan (2016, 36) puts it, "Leadership potential emerges when others recognize, support, and make space for our unique gifts, strengths, and contributions." We are continuously in need of strong leaders in the nonprofit world and in the ECE field. We need champions who will continue to lead the cause on behalf of children and families. From the classroom and program level, to the city, state, and national level, we need to uncover and support leadership talent and strengths. There is much work to be done, and there is room for all leaders with diverse skills, strengths, and interests. Look for those who have a vision or think systemically. Notice those who take initiative or challenge assumptions. Let these people know you notice them, and help them see the leadership skills they have and can use.

Nurturing Others' Strengths

As leaders, our role is sometimes to help other leaders in their journey. All of us probably had a time when someone gave us a leg up. We have probably all had people in our lives who recognized our potential and provided opportunities for us to gain experience and expand our leadership skills. As leaders, it's our turn to give others a hand with their leadership opportunities. Think of ways you can nurture others' strengths. Look for opportunities where others can take the lead on a task or step up during a meeting. Perhaps the strengths or great skills of an up-and-coming leader would be a perfect fit for a particular project or some aspect of a project.

Letting Go So Others May Lead

To give people opportunities to lead, one needs to do just that—give them opportunities to lead. Sometimes this means trusting others' abilities, strengths, and ideas. It may mean letting go of your way of doing something and getting out of others' way so they can go forward with their own leadership goals and see their own ideas through. Everyone has strengths and skills, and people can assume acts of leadership from various roles and positions.

Sometimes Leaders Should Get Out of the Way

One of my favorite phrases that I hear my staff say is, "I got this." To me, this is a wonderful example of leadership. One of my leadership philosophies is to hire good people, support their emerging leadership skills, and then get out of their way. I try to bring together individuals and team members who have the knowledge and skills to do their jobs well, or the aptitudes and skill-building abilities to jump in and gather the additional knowledge and skills needed to do the job. As a leader, I believe it is my job to make sure they have the information, resources, and support to succeed in their jobs. I nurture their strengths by giving feedback and by being transparent about successes and challenges. Then I let them have the autonomy to take some leadership and see the work through.

These individuals begin to build their own programs, systems, or ways of doing things that work for them and their team. They build skills, they have successes, and when they need to check in and get ideas, guidance, or assistance, I make myself available. What I have seen is that often they have skills and strengths I didn't know about or that I myself don't have. They have ideas that I would never have thought of. And sometimes I have ideas they didn't think of. We build on one another's strengths and are able to do things better than I can do alone as a leader. And not long after, when I go to one of these individuals with something that needs to be done, or something I thought about or am concerned about, she or he will turn to me with a smile and say, "Yeah, I know. I got this."

Part II

Building Collaboration

CHAPTER 3

What Is Collaboration, and Why Do It?

COLLABORATION. It's a word we hear more and more in the work world. More funders are seeking or even requiring collaborative projects in their proposal requests. Increasingly, businesses and agencies are trying to collaborate to better reach or serve their target populations. Some organizations try collaborations as a way to shift work culture or operate more effectively. But what does it really mean to collaborate? What are the benefits of collaborating, and how can an organization embark on this work?

Definitions of Collaboration

Collaboration begins when people work together toward a common goal and achieve something they couldn't have done as well if they had been working alone. Collaboration does not just involve the way agencies are organized or networked, it is more about the way they work together. It is a cooperative effort involving extensive resource sharing, significant time commitment, decision making, and mutual trust to see the process through to fruition.

Collaboration is a more extensive and deeper commitment than coordinating services or programs or cooperating on projects. Collaboration is on the high end of the continuum of possible ways to work across agencies and to develop systems-level work. It involves greater time commitment, increased resource sharing, and shared leadership, authority, or governance.

It is not necessarily the best way to work together, but it is the most intense and integrated way to work together and may be the best model for the work you want to accomplish.

Table 3.1

INCREASING INTENSITY →

Cooperation	Coordination	Collaboration
Sharing ideas or information to help each other	Sharing approaches to deliver services to achieve a common purpose	Commitment to deliver, align, or integrate services and programs together with shared authority, mission, goals, and resources

Collaboration can refer to a group of people within one organization or cross-organizational collaboration in which multiple separate organizations, or individuals participating on their behalf, work together toward a common purpose. Collaboration has been written about and used across multiple organizations, sectors, and fields. Authors across various disciplines have contributed to the ideas and definitions of collaboration. As David Straus (2002, 5), an experienced leader and founder of Interaction Associates, Inc., defines it, collaboration is "the process people employ when working together in a group, organization, or community to plan, create, solve problems, and make decisions."

Organizational development consultant Joan M. Roberts (2010, 6) defines collaboration as "a group of people working together to reach a common goal." Russell M. Linden (2002, 7), a management educator who specializes in organizational change, takes this one step further: "Collaboration occurs when people from different organizations (or units within one organization) produce something together through joint effort, resources, and decision-making, and share ownership of the final product or service." Both authors agree that working together and sharing resources to achieve the common goal of producing a joint product are key components of collaboration.

In their book, *Collaboration Handbook: Creating, Sustaining, and Enjoying the Journey,* Michael Winer and Karen Ray (1994, 24) define collaboration as a "mutually beneficial and well-defined relationship entered into by two or more organizations to achieve results they are more likely to achieve together than alone." Here the emphasis is on the common goal or mutual benefit *and* on the well-defined relationship between collaborators. In addition, Winer and Ray agree that a significant component of collaboration is that it is work that must be done together with others because the goal cannot be met adequately by one individual or one agency working alone.

Collaboration is about creating value, not just a final product or a service. Communication and collaboration strategist Evan Rosen (2007, 9) defines collaboration as "working together to create value while sharing virtual or physical space." He adds mention of virtual space because often collaboration happens between collaborators who are working in different locations. Collaboration can be among those in the same field and in the same place or can occur across fields and in different locations. According to Rosen (2007, 9), "Collaboration transcends hierarchy, education, field, function, and location."

Why Collaborate?

The work of collaboration is to produce or implement something to better address issues or deliver better services, outcomes, or products to achieve a common goal. As Linden and others note, the goal isn't collaboration for its own sake, but to work together to produce or deliver better service, outcomes, or products for clients, stakeholders, or communities. The focus is on a common goal to produce or implement something to better address issues. What is also significant is that the end result of collaboration is shared ownership of the efforts, services, and products. The outcomes belong to all. The results are not yours or mine, but ours.

Collaboration is the new imperative. It's the only way to accelerate innovation, improve agility, increase adaptability, and cut costs all at once. —Ron Ricci and Carl Wiese

Collaboration is transformational. It can and will change the way organizations work, both individually and collectively. Collaboration can help when organizations find themselves stuck in a rut and new ideas or new ways of addressing issues are needed. Or perhaps new services or a new way of delivering those services would better serve clients or communities. As Kagan and Kauerz (2012, 5) point out, "Whether dubbed systems efforts, partnerships, linkages, coordination, or collaboration, such efforts are designed to stimulate new thinking and new actions that will expand services, improve their qualities and outcomes, and reduce inequities in access."

For example, in 2007 the leaders of the BUILD Initiative were trying to find ways to connect those working in different states across the country so they could help each other create coordinated early childhood systems. The BUILD Initiative began a collaboration with Smart Start in North Carolina to launch a national movement with the shared goal of making quality rating and improvement systems–related research available to help move ideas and connect policy and practice. As Gerrit Westervelt explains, the two organizations ambitiously "rolled up their sleeves together" and the result was the QRIS National Learning Network (pers. comm.). This enabled the BUILD Initiative to provide nationwide support for QRIS and developed a way for leaders across the country to think together to address issues and expand their services to better address the needs of communities.

In a chapter for *Early Learning Systems*, Dean Clifford (2012, 165) notes that "collaboration among many stakeholders is essential for success in early childhood system building. Collaboration brings together a wealth of expertise and in-kind resources that, together, can have greater impact and influence than the expertise and resources of any single organization." Collaboration can expand or improve services, better achieve outcomes, or reduce barriers and inequities in accessing services.

Collaboration is important not just because it's a better way to learn. The spirit of collaboration is penetrating every institution and all our lives. So learning to collaborate is part of equipping yourself for effectiveness, problem solving, innovation and lifelong learning in an ever-changing networked economy.
—Don Tapscott

Reasons to Collaborate

The ECE field is a natural fit for collaborative projects. Sometimes to best serve a child, family, or community, multiple stakeholders need to figure out how to work together. Furthermore, with greater national, state, and local attention paid to the importance of ECE, the time is right for agencies, organizations, and institutions to examine how to work more collaboratively.

Changing Culture and Nature of Work

Societal challenges and work environments are more complex than ever. Due to technological advances, the world is changing. We are more connected than ever before, making it even easier to work collaboratively than it was in the past. More information is readily available, and new knowledge now moves at a much faster pace. Therefore, how work flows through and between individuals and organizations has also changed. Rosen (2007, 1) notes, "At work, information used to arrive in our in-baskets, later in our email in-boxes. We received instructions and passed them to others. Somebody else had to do their part before we could do ours." But now technology allows for collaborative efforts across broad geographic areas and service areas, using new delivery types and modes of communication such as email, webinars, Google docs, or other shared platforms.

Information moves more quickly, and decisions can be made more efficiently and more comprehensively. Information is available whenever, wherever, and however we need it, which allows us to interact with others about it almost as soon as we receive it. With multiple ways to meet and instantaneously share documents and information, the barriers to working together are greatly reduced.

As a result, problem solving and decision-making in today's world is made easier as people are able to meet in real time via Skype or FaceTime when issues arise. This model requires supportive, interactive environments that cultivate collaboration.

Complexity of Today's Challenges

The issues facing today's children and families, as well as the agencies that serve them, are often multilayered and complex. Early childhood and nonprofit organizations routinely deal with the issues of poverty, homelessness, violence and crime, and abuse and neglect among children and families. At the same time, programs must stay up to date on changing education standards, regulations, and new research or approaches. Tackling these issues and serving children and families in current times requires innovative thinking and new approaches to problem solving. Working with other organizations that offer different services or programs in new ways provides better opportunities to meet the complex challenges facing families.

Working Together to Keep Families Healthy

When the Los Angeles County Department of Public Health (DPH) sought to increase the number of flu and pertussis immunizations given, the agency discovered that by partnering with child care resource and referral (R&R) agencies, it would be able to more broadly and effectively reach out to children and families in the community. The R&Rs reached out to the families they worked with directly and gave information to child care providers to share with the families they serve. Within a few months, community-based clinics were set up at the R&Rs. At those clinics, more than 1,800 people received flu vaccinations, more than 1,600 pertussis shots were administered, and information on the importance of immunizations was distributed to more than 30,000 parents and 18,000 child care providers (Wold and Associates 2011).

When the DPH later received funding to focus on early childhood obesity, the organization again turned to a collaborative approach. Building on the R&Rs' ongoing work and trusted relationships with child care providers and parents, the project reached 3,143 child care providers and 30,633 families, providing training, information, resources and/or support on healthy nutrition and physical activity practices (Child Care Resource Center 2017). Additional collaborative partners included health providers, local nonprofits serving families, food assistance programs, farm to preschool programs, local grocery stores, and other community-based organizations. The Department of Public Health also partnered with breastfeeding promotion programs, local restaurants, and others to meet this complex challenge in multilayered ways. Thanks to these collaborative efforts, information about the issue of childhood obesity was distributed using a comprehensive network of services and approaches.

Public Demand for Improved Performance and Services

Increasingly, the public and funding sources are holding organizations accountable for meeting deliverables and goals, requiring that programs document results to demonstrate achieved outcomes. Some funding sources even require collaboration in order for an organization to be eligible to receive funds. With greater access to information on what constitutes quality services, parents and community members are empowered to seek out such quality and hold programs accountable for adhering to these standards. And this demand now moves at the speed of the internet and social media. Organizations must be ready to respond to questions with thoughtful solutions.

Through established collaborations, organizations have the additional knowledge and flexibility to meet community needs with improved, cost-effective services at a more rapid pace. And, since collaboration is always adapting and evolving, as new challenges arise, other collaborations can form to address those needs.

Opportunities for Leadership and New Leadership Styles

Leadership development is critically important in the ECE field and for nonprofits in general. The field is facing a potential shortage in leaders as people retire or transition in their work. Now is the time to both cultivate and prepare future leaders for new ways of working together. True collaboration requires innovative and motivated leaders who are determined, committed, and collaborative, and who hold inclusive values. Collaborations in and of themselves provide many opportunities to identify and foster emerging leaders as well as further develop more experienced leaders. Through collaborative projects, leaders with the passion, perseverance, and vision to shape and transform the future will have the opportunity to add to their skills and knowledge.

Collaboration Assessment

Think about the issues or challenges facing your organization. Is collaboration a possible solution? Here are some questions to help you assess if a collaborative effort is needed:

- What are the challenges in your community?
- How might you address these challenges?
- How can you do so while keeping your organization fiscally viable?
- What are possible solutions? How might you achieve these in meaningful ways?

- Are the solutions attainable? If so, are they sustainable?
- Are the solutions cost-effective?

- Who needs to be involved in this work?
  - Are there individuals or organizations you have worked with in the past that might be a good fit for this project?
  - Are you already working with these individuals or organizations? Do you have the necessary relationships?
  - Who is missing from the project?

Benefits of Collaboration

Collaborating comes with many benefits. Although working collaboratively with others takes work and perseverance, the benefits to you and your organization are worth the effort. Working collaboratively can result in greater impact and more effectively achieve systems-level goals.

Cost-Effective Use of Scarce Resources

Nonprofit organizations often face a scarcity of resources, a problem that intensified during the recession years. Many organizations, including several that serve children and families, found it increasingly difficult to carry out their work or even continue to operate during this time. Under these conditions, organizations found new and different ways to complete their goals. Collaborative models were one way. These models can create opportunities to address economies-of-scale issues or to streamline and use resources more effectively.

Collaboration Leads to Greater Possibilities

Organizations can't respond to every type of need or deliver every type of service. For an agency to survive fiscally and stay relevant, it must find a way to stay true to the mission within fiscal limitations. Reaching far beyond an organization's core services, mission, or budget can be very risky. Often it makes more sense to continue to do what the organization does well. But working together with other agencies provides opportunities to blend, combine, extend, or leverage other services into a single system or program. Think of it as the stone soup approach to solving community problems or creating comprehensive systems. Each agency brings its strengths and services to the endeavor to create something bigger and better than one single entity could. To tackle a problem affecting families or to create a program to better serve children, collaborative efforts tend to allow for a more comprehensive approach.

Early Childhood Literacy

One local community collaborative formed when multiple organizations worked together to address early childhood literacy in a systemic way. A local college provided courses on Early Childhood Literacy for ECE teachers. The child care R&R provided ECE coaches, who also served as teaching assistants in the course, to work with the participants at their child care sites to support integrating what was learned in the courses into practice. The local Head Start agency and public library provided lending libraries, storytellers, and literacy activities at the child care sites to enhance the learning environment. A community agency that serves children with learning disabilities provided information on working with children with special needs and consultation for participating child care providers with children that needed additional literacy support. Over time, this collaboration resulted in several hundred child care professionals gaining six units in early childhood literacy courses; hundreds of child care programs getting on-site support with books, literacy activities and materials, and storytelling; and hundreds of families visiting the library, getting library cards, and engaging in literacy activities.

Higher Quality and More Integrated Service or Products

We want to serve our children, families, and clients with the highest quality service. Sometimes the best way to do that is to work with others to provide a more seamless, networked delivery of services. This allows the client to benefit from the leveraged resources and more integrated services or programs, sometimes without even knowing about the many levels of collaboration at work behind the scenes. This also allows for a more mission-driven approach to service delivery. What drives the programs and how people benefit is the intent behind the collaboration. The high quality of the service or product is the focus and the reason the collaboration comes together.

Increased Ability to Achieve Necessary or Important Outcomes

Sometimes a collaboration forms to reach important outcomes that are better or more easily met when a collective group approaches the issues. What strategies or activities will lead to better outcomes for the children and families in your programs? Perhaps your community is facing issues of poverty, homelessness, low literacy rates, high obesity rates, or other socioeconomic or health disparities. Striving toward better outcomes for children and families is often better done when a cross-organization or even cross-sector approach is used to more effectively leverage knowledge, resources, ideas, infrastructures, and talents.

Greater Organization Efficiency and Greater Content Knowledge

The corporate world has already been learning that the ability to build and maintain collaborative relationships is an important skill and asset among its employees. These skills can be as important as the intellectual or financial capital of the company because they add knowledge through the collective wisdom of those collaborating together. The world is constantly changing and continuously striving toward greater efficiencies. Increased knowledge will keep your organization strong and ready to meet the needs of your community.

Levels of Collaboration

Like systems-building work, collaboration can happen at all levels. Perhaps within your classroom, program, or organization, there are ways that collaboration can help achieve a goal or address a challenge. On a broader level, collaboration may help improve services across sectors or align systems for greater efficiencies. Wherever there is something to accomplish that would be done better together with others, there is an opportunity for collaboration.

Local Level

At the local level, collaborations can be built within an agency or with partner agencies in the same community. Think of the organizations in your area that are doing similar or related work. Look to the agencies trying to make a difference with the same target populations. Consider those agencies with which you have relationships already. Are there ways those connections might be expanded to include working together to solve issues? Collaboration opportunities could arise from within a program (across classroom and age groups), with parents or community members, across multiple programs within a single agency or entity, or from a cross agency (same type of services) or cross sector within the local community (different or complementing/aligning services).

Regional Level

There may be opportunities for collaborations to expand across a county, or perhaps entire region, of a state. Building on or expanding into the systems within which your programs or agencies operate can provide opportunities to take a collaboration to scale or increase the impact and/or outcomes of the work. Consider the networks, systems, or sectors within which your programs or agencies exist. Perhaps there are opportunities to expand your collaborative efforts to include these larger regional levels through cross-agency or cross-sector work throughout a region, multiservice delivery coordination, or alignment of services and/or programs.

State Level

Collaboration at the state level can lead to projects, initiatives, or systems change that can affect programs across the state. State-level collaboration requires working within or across state departments, agencies, or sectors to build models, programs, or systems that could influence statewide projects or even create infrastructure or foundational components for the field, such as funding models, state ECE systems plans, child care access and subsidy systems, quality improvement or QRIS systems, professional development/career ladder systems, and higher education systems and/or alignment. Collaboration at the state level will require relationship building, planning, and work at the state department or agency level. State-level work may also require working with state legislators or advocates.

Possible Issues to Address through Collaboration

Think of common goals you and others have to improve services or address issues for children and families at your organization or in your community. Below is a sample list of the types of issues that could be addressed through a collaborative, systems-building approach:

- **health disparities**—physical health, mental health, dental health, access to health care
- **nutrition**—access to healthy food, obesity reduction, access to information, nutrition policy improvements
- **special needs and inclusion**—identification, referrals, access to services, training for service providers
- **literacy**—access to high-quality literature, improved reading levels, libraries
- **housing and homelessness**—access to shelters, referrals to services

- **child care access**—subsidy programs, access for children in foster care
- **child care quality**—improving the environments, interactions, and practices in child care settings
- **workforce development**—access to education and professional development training, mentoring or coaching, preservice preparation
- **ECE workforce compensation**—systems and/or initiatives aimed at improving ECE professionals' wages and benefits

CHAPTER 4

Collaborative Leadership: What Works

IN *THE COLLABORATION IMPERATIVE: Executive Strategies for Unlocking Your Organization's True Potential*, Ron Ricci and Carl Wiese (2011, 33) point out, "There is no cookie-cutter approach to developing collaborative processes. All organizations—even ones in the same industry—are unique. Each one needs to assess its distinct business processes to determine where increased collaboration can drive improvement." In other words, collaboration is a journey among and between individuals and organizations. This means each collaborative effort will be unique depending on the community's problems, needs, resources, strengths, and challenges. It might also depend on the type and mix of organizations collaborating. For example, a large bureaucratic organization and a nonprofit might have very different hierarchical structures, operational styles, and service delivery modes. So before you begin, it is important to assess the readiness of the organizations and individuals with regard to the work ahead.

As with anything one develops, starting with the basics will help establish a solid foundation on which to build. Before launching a collaborative, determine if this is the right time, these are the right organizations, and you are embarking on this work for the right reasons.

Key Elements of Collaboration

Before beginning to collaborate, reflect on the following ideas. Ask if you and your organization have done the following (Linden 2002):

- agreed that there is a reason or shared interest that all interested parties want to pursue at this time
- discussed the interests of each potential and the goals for this process
- defined what each individual/organization brings to the collaboration and/or process
- brought together those who can represent the views of each stakeholder organization
- identified and supported those who will serve as leaders and/or champions for this work or process
- considered how the process will be managed or led
- thought through the potential impact if the initiative succeeds
- begun to establish trusting relationships and started to get to know each other

Thinking through these points will help identify the shared interests and potential partners for the work. This process will also provide the opportunity to see if the shared interests are strong enough and if there is enough buy-in from the potential partners. Considering each of these points will also allow time to identify potential leaders and to begin to think through possible processes and strategies. Relationships can be built throughout this process. But most collaborations are based on existing relationships. For collaborations to grow and succeed, the levels of trust in either newly built or existing relationships must be nurtured, maintained, and increased. Working on building this trust from the beginning is an important and helpful investment.

Some organizations may drop out of the work because they do not find it a good match or because the context in which they work does not support a collaborative effort. It is best to identify this somewhat early on in the process so as not to hinder the collaborative work going forward. Checking in on these key elements from the onset and periodically throughout the process will help build a productive and successful collaboration.

Individual Collaboration Skills

Although collaboration is about multiple organizations, agencies, or people working together, it is important to think about what works by starting with the individuals who will be seeing this work through. Having individuals who are committed to collaboration and who possess the right skills and dispositions for collaborative work is vital. James W. Tamm and Ronald J. Luyet (2004, 8) believe that collaboration must begin with individuals, not organizations: "Without collaborative skills, a team is just a group of individuals who each follow their own agenda." Including individuals with strong collaboration skills and promoting opportunities to learn and build these skills is imperative.

What individual skills are necessary for successful collaboration? Tamm and Luyet assert that there are five essential skills to realize true collaboration: collaborative intention, truthfulness, self-accountability, self-awareness and awareness of others, and problem solving and negotiating. I would add that integrity, dedication to high-quality service, and openness to change and transformation are essential to collaboration as well.

To be open to change, one must be genuinely interested in the ideas and viewpoints of others and in the possibility of being changed by what one hears or learns. This requires the self-awareness that Tamm and Luyet speak of as well as the self-confidence to be okay with different or new ideas and views. To be open to other ideas also requires listening intently, being interested in different viewpoints, and having the desire to seek knowledge and understanding. Therefore, dedication to open communication and being receptive to feedback are critical components in the collaborative process.

Openness to change also requires an acceptance that conflict is a natural part of working toward transformation and change. Therefore, problem-solving and negotiating skills and the desire to generate ideas and seek solutions are critical to collaborations. One must be comfortable working through conflict while staying focused and dedicated to the process and to high-quality results. Each individual must be willing to let the collaborative process and the collective impact rise above individual ideas, needs, or goals. This takes a good deal of honesty, self-awareness, self-confidence, and trust.

Trusting Relationships

Building trusting relationships at the onset of a collaboration is essential. As Linden (2002, 94) explains, "Poor relationships will kill almost any alliance; without strong relationships there's not trust, and without trust there will be no collaboration." With trust people will be willing to work together toward common goals and take risks. To truly collaborate also may include letting go of some control and making compromises and difficult decisions. This is easier to do if you trust that others have the best intentions and collectively want the best for the greater good.

Another reason trusting relationships are critical for a successful collaboration is that the journey may be long or full of many twists, turns, challenges, and unknowns. The group will need to be able to work through these challenges together. Collaborative partners need to trust and support each other through good times and bad. The collaborative journey may also include some tough conversations about roles, funds, values, methods and models, and more. Trusting relationships will help enable collaboration members to openly and honestly have these discussions.

In the ECE field, as in many other nonprofit or value-driven fields, people understand the importance of relationships. Team members willingly collaborate on issues they feel passionate about. This degree of passion and dedication can't be mandated or bought. It will be there in the determination and spirit of those working together toward a cause they believe in. But for all to continue to bring their best selves, their passion, and their enthusiasm to the collaborative process, trust must be present.

Key Elements of Trust

The ability for all collaborators to remain open and vigilant to key elements of trust will allow the group to increasingly grow relationships and maintain trust throughout the process. Trust has four key elements:

- active listening to all opinions and beliefs
- willingness to be open to new ideas
- valuing of all contributions
- honoring all knowledge and expertise

How to Build It or How to Rebuild It If It Gets Lost

Collaborative leaders and members can work together to build trust. All leaders and members must agree to put forth themselves and their ideas while continuing to strive toward the collective goals. Doing this requires trusting one another to listen and value the ideas of all collaborators. All must agree to honor the knowledge, wisdom, and expertise that each individual brings to the process. It is okay to have different ideas or opinions, but all group members must endeavor to suspend judgment and be open to hearing new information and learning from others.

How to Build Trust

- Be transparent—Keep everyone informed and make decisions with others or ensure that all are informed of decisions.
- Act with integrity—Be honest in words and deeds and make sure actions and decisions are in line with values.
- Be dependable—Provide stability by being dependable and consistent so everyone knows you can be counted on.
- Keep promises—Make sure to follow through on responsibilities and commitments.
- Listen—Take in what others share and make it a goal to learn from others.
- Be open— Encourage participation and appreciate different viewpoints and ideas.
- Maintain confidence—Be loyal and reliable to group members and with shared information.
- Honor values—Hold yourself and group members accountable to group values and agreed-upon guidelines and standards.
- Be professional—Speak and act in calm and respectful ways.

(Marotz and Lawson 2007)

Trust may get lost along the way. Collaborative work isn't always easy, and it can take a long time. Sometimes personal and organization needs and interests compete for time, goals, or outcomes. Focusing on trust from the beginning will reduce this. Plan for and establish trust as early in the collaborative process as possible. And have ideas, plans, and methods for monitoring and rebuilding trust if it should erode at any point in the process.

Setting up ways to check in with members of the collaboration and to continuously gauge trust and commitment levels is important. This should be done both formally and informally throughout the collaborative systems-building process:

- **Informal**—As part of the collaborative process, establish some kind of regular check-in. Perhaps there is a standing item on each agenda or a trust-building/monitoring activity that takes place each quarter. Be honest, up-front, and transparent about this. Perhaps even go around the room and do a check-in with each partner to make sure he or she is still in.
- **Formal**—It may be really important to establish formal Memorandums of Understanding (MOU) or form an agreement with each collaborative partner. This document should spell out the details of the collaborative effort and what each partner is committing to in regard to time and resources. It should also spell out the collective goals and vision of the group and the intended outcomes.

If any partner begins to lose trust or others lose trust in one of the partners or partnering organizations, the collaboration will be jeopardized. This is a key time to listen and learn from each other about what the trust issues may be. Then together, in an open and transparent process, the group can work through the trust issues, determine how to address them, and decide on the next steps. Keeping the focus on the goals and the vision will help. This shouldn't be about individual people or individual organizations but about the interest, time, ability, and commitment to seeing the process through together.

If at any point an organization decides it can't fully participate or put the common interests or goals of the collaboration ahead of organizational interests, then that organization needs say so and step away from the effort. This is completely okay. The collaborative partners need to ensure that all organizations feel that it is safe to withdraw from the group and that such situations will be handled honestly and with transparency.

The Bay Area Consortium

The Bay Area QRIS Partnership is a consortium of five counties in the California San Francisco Bay Area (Alameda, Contra Costa, San Francisco, Santa Clara, and Santa Cruz). They came together with funding from the federal Race to the Top–Early Learning Challenge grants and a regional goal to develop and implement a QRIS. The counties are working together with a common vision and approach for child care quality improvement. The collaborative partners "are leveraging their experiences and lessons learned in developing their local QRIS's to identify opportunities to coordinate their work, more efficiently use resources, and otherwise create a common approach and movement for quality improvement across the Bay Area Region" (First 5 Santa Clara County, accessed 2017).

Early in the process, the counties recognized the importance of maintaining strong relationships, building trust, and coming together around a collective vision. One successful strategy was to develop a governance structure and allocate appropriate resources to coordinate the process, including working with a facilitator. According to Jolene Smith (pers. comm.), chief executive officer of First 5 Santa Clara County, the process included hands-on leadership. The collaborative partners worked hard to develop an ecological and noncompetitive view. Doing so took time, and there were "hard conversations about how to work together." Smith stresses that the key to collaborative work is to "let go of individual interests and shift to the greater good of the group." She spoke of this process as a "release of self" and of developing "unconditional positive regard" for collaborative partners to work toward the common vision "because you know it's the right thing to do." As one of the partnership's reports (Bay Area Quality Early Learning Partnership 2015, 5) states, the collaborative process "required continual balancing of regional versus county-level interests and needs, as each has its own budget, infrastructure, and consortium with specific goals and priorities." The collaborative was ultimately successful because of the structured and multilevel approach to governance and decision-making, the dedication to common goals and vision, the desire to increase operational and financial efficiencies, the willingness to share resources, and the strengths of leveraging expertise across the multiple counties.

Valuing Strengths of Each Agency

Each individual and agency has strengths. Successful collaborations place value in the different strengths each entity brings and determine ways to build on or include them. Each individual person and agency has unique and interesting skills to offer. A truly collaborative process will allow opportunities for all to learn about these skills and think through the best strategies and designs to use them. Sometimes that may mean recognizing that another agency is better at something than your agency. It may mean letting go of how you thought the process might unfold.

One example of this is a higher-education collaboration in California comprised of child development faculty from public and private colleges and universities. The collaborative's focus is on strengthening higher education systems to support the building of aligned academic and professional development pathways for the ECE workforce. From the onset, "PEACH (Partnerships for Education, Articulation and Coordination through Higher Education) created a forum that recognizes the strengths and value of each voice at the table by building relationships through collaborative work, respecting and embracing each individual's pace, perspective, and style while co-constructing shared vision and accomplishing common goals. They value listening, sharing, working together and accomplishing goals together because both relationships *and* work deepen through this process" (Jan Fish, pers. comm.). At the local level, the collaborative has articulated coursework and programs and worked together to develop ECE baccalaureate and doctoral programs. At the state level, it has advocated for the development of an ECE teaching credential.

Agreement on Purpose, Vision, and Goals

Coming to some agreement on purpose, vision, and goals early in the collaborative process is important. Without agreement on the reasons for working together or an understanding of the common goals, collaborators can become frustrated and decide not to fully participate. There has to be shared understanding of the purpose and buy-in for people to truly engage and participate. Many of us have sat in meetings that seemed to have no clear agenda or goals. I know I have felt like such meetings are not only a waste of my time, but I don't have a clear understanding of why I'm there. When this happens, people begin to feel as if their ideas don't matter or that there is no strong or compelling reason to participate. On the other hand, when I've been part of coming up with the purpose, vision, and goals, I feel a sense of ownership in the project. I feel connected to the process and more dedicated to seeing it through.

Collaboration is a journey. It begins when people work together toward a common goal and achieve something they couldn't have done as well on their own. It can have amazing benefits and provide wonderful opportunities to build new, successful programs or address ongoing issues in different ways. It can also allow for new leadership and growth opportunities. But it can be challenging and hard work. It may require rolling up one's sleeves with the desire to persevere through adversity and work toward solutions. One must have the will to approach problems in new ways and to seek out and be open to diverse opinions. Collaboration requires honesty, integrity, and the willingness to listen, learn, and value new ideas.

True collaboration requires integrity. Entering into collaborative work with the best of intentions is critical. But collaboration also requires honesty and humbleness. To truly be open to collaboration, one must be steadfast and true to the values of working through challenges and problems together. One must also be dedicated to a process and journey filled with different ideas, opinions, styles, and approaches. Collaborators must endeavor to discover the best solution, even if it differs from what was done before or deviates from what was previously thought.

But successful collaboration is possible, and it will be a critical and valuable way to approach societal and work issues going forward. Coming to this work with steadfast resolve, commitment, and thought will strengthen all collaborative efforts and lead to greater individual professional growth.

Part III

Leadership in Action

CHAPTER 5

The Planning Stage

SYSTEMS-BUILDING and systems-change work requires a lot of planning. The work is complicated, and it will be important to start with an understanding of the issues you are trying to solve and then step-by-step work through all aspects of addressing the challenges and solving the problem. This takes time, persistence, invested stakeholders and participants, and a process and structure. This chapter will provide information on how to define and clarify the problem, include participation, and begin to build a framework and determine actionable steps.

Understanding the Problem

To begin working on change, one must first understand the problem. What needs changing? What are the challenges? What are the parts of the system that need improving, and in what bigger picture or context do they operate? Understanding the bigger picture and contributing factors as well as the details of the problem is key to understanding the systemic changes necessary for improvement.

Define and Clarify the Problem

Although the problem may seem obvious, people can come to the collaborative systems-building process with different views on what the underlying or fundamental problem may be. It is essential to clarify, agree upon, and define the problem early on. What exactly are you trying to improve or address? There may be multiple issues, in which case it will be necessary to tease them apart:

- **Assessing current system(s) characteristics**—It will be important to first assess the structure and characteristics of the current system. The planning process needs to be informed by current designs, policies, and contexts. What is the current reality and how is it helping or hindering progress? What organizational structures or systems increase or inhibit impact?
- **Critical assessment questions**—Determine the questions that need to be asked. What do you need to know to define and clarify the problem? How could you assess the specific issues? What is working? What is not working? What needs improvement?

To truly understand and clarify what needs work, one needs to reflect on it from different vantage points. When working to define the problem, consider the issues from various perspectives. Addressing all the underlying issues requires understanding the impact at all levels. This means following up and communicating with all individuals who are involved in the work in different ways and at various levels.

Include Diverse Stakeholders

Including diverse stakeholders in the process is crucial. People from different backgrounds, perspectives, positions, abilities, roles, organizations, and sectors should be part of clarifying, defining, and solving problems. This requires commitment and planning to ensure accessible representation. All involved must consider who is not there and why, and then take steps to make sure those missing have a seat at the table.

Lea J. E. Austin (pers. comm.) from the Center for the Study of Child Care Employment (CSCCE) explains why inclusion is so important: "It is insufficient to have only one or two people represent diversity." Being in a room full of people, none of whom are like you "can still silence a community," she adds. Truly including diverse stakeholders is not just making sure people who have been labeled a certain way are in the room. Leaders must work to create a safe space and ensure that all who are included have a voice and that each voice is meaningful.

Vertical and Horizontal Representation and Participation

To avoid perpetuating inequities or systematized oppression, including those directly affected by the decisions or issues at play is imperative. Often decisions are made at higher systems levels—by statewide governing or deciding bodies, government regulators, or policy makers through legislation. These decisions often include funding amounts and how resources will be used and distributed.

Making sure that meeting times are accessible is a key part of inclusion. To ensure parents can attend, the meetings need to be held at a time when and in a location where parents are available. Parents may also need child care in order to participate in meetings. If it is crucial for ECE staff to give their opinions and ideas, then the meetings will also need to be accessible to them. Transportation or language interpretation services and translated documents may also be critical to ensure that people can engage in conversation and read meeting materials.

Improving the chances for full participation also involves thinking ahead about the structure of meetings. Make sure that meeting agendas, communication models, and decision-making processes not only include information learned from various perspectives but also encourage all to contribute ideas and solutions, and to help make decisions. People must have a voice but also should be involved in determining ways to improve the systems that affect their lives.

Explore and Understand Different Perspectives

The commitment to include diverse stakeholders begins with a dedication to seek out and understand various perspectives. Part of the planning process should be to incorporate ways to ask critical questions and gain insight and understanding about how the programs, systems, or issues are viewed or perceived by all involved. To truly understand and define the problem requires seeing it with a different lens and exploring it from all sides. Keep in mind that there is no one way to see things and no right or wrong way to experience or be affected by current issues. Understanding this enables the process to be more inclusive and truly address issues in more equitable ways.

Principles for System Planning

Having principles to guide systems-planning work is a necessity. These grounding principles help all involved to stay focused on how the work will be done. Based on work done at the National Center for Children & Families at Teachers College, Columbia University, authors Sharon Lynn Kagan, Kate Tarrant, and Kristie Kauerz outlined five principles they believe are key to ECE systems planning. The authors' work focuses primarily on the state level, but these principles could be applied to systems building at different levels.

Champion Inclusivity and Transparency

As mentioned earlier, the process must be inclusive. But it must also be transparent to all involved, including other stakeholders and those affected by any decisions or outcomes. People need to know what is being worked on and how. There should be transparency with regard to what the process is working to achieve, the activities of the planning process, the timelines, the decisions made, and any accomplishments or deliverables.

Use Current Research and Adopt a Theory of Change

For the planning to be successful and impactful, it should be based on current research and reflect all the information and data available about best practices. The process should not only be guided by the field's best thinking and research, but it should also be future thinking, striving for progress in the months and years to come. The whole process should be driven by a theory of change with an ultimate goal of better outcomes for children and families. By embracing change from the beginning and actively planning and working toward that goal, the end result will be an improvement on the current reality.

Account for Current Realities and Context

Although the planning process should be future thinking, it also needs to factor in the current situation. Systems exist within political and social contexts, and planning processes need to be informed by those in order to build on them or exist within them. Understanding the policies, financial structures, governance issues, and administrative practices that influence or drive how this work could be carried out is vital. In addition, planning must factor in the public and political interest and support for the work. The level of societal knowledge and/or support on the issues will influence how this work is carried out, how the planning process responds, and how it either builds on or increases public will.

Create Actionable Next Steps

To maintain commitment and active participation, the planning process must be making progress. Planning should lead to both short-term and long-term goals with accomplishments along the way. Priorities should be identified, including some priorities that are actionable in the short term. And to be actionable, the identified steps need to be feasible. To continue to build momentum, it's important to determine what is possible and build in incremental successes along the way.

Develop an Ongoing Process

The process shouldn't end when all the planning is done. Whatever plans, systems, activities, or programs are implemented should be continuously monitored and assessed. There should be an articulated plan to oversee, revisit, modify, and update the plans and products as needed. The systems-building efforts should be sustainable, and plans should include governance, oversight, and continuous monitoring over time. In this underresourced and fragmented field, it should be understood that change is a given and the planning and systems-building efforts may be ongoing for years to come. Time, resources, additional planning, and systems-building will be needed to realize truly sustainable systems-level change.

Develop a Framework

A framework provides a way to organize the process and to articulate and guide the work. Often organized as a table or logic model, a framework documents and reinforces the change that will take place. And, for the broader community, it can illustrate the macro-level systems work that is taking place. A framework keeps everyone unified and aligned with the vision and goals and maintains a focus on the greater purpose. A framework can include program or infrastructure focus areas, goals, outcomes, strategies, and activities. A framework should achieve the following actions:

- build on a common vision
- articulate guiding principles
- provide common language
- display agreed-upon goals
- describe desired outcomes
- promote accountability
- encourage commitment to results

When developing a framework in Colorado, Jeanine Coleman and Jodi Hardin (2012, 219) wrote of the need of early childhood partners in the state to "synthesize and integrate multiple years' system-building efforts into a plan that would provide a collective vision, guide next steps in systems work, and link system-building efforts to outcomes." A framework was developed to document and guide the work, and that framework has been updated and revised over the years.

Developing a Framework to Guide the Work

In Palm Beach County, Florida, Tanya Palmer and Michelle Gross of the Children's Services Council developed a framework called the Pathway to Early Childhood Development. The Children's Services Council is the backbone and funding agency of the county's QRIS. Palmer and Gross said the process of creating a framework helped them distill the system down to the major strategies and main talking points. They felt this was essential not only to provide the broader context of the work but also to clearly articulate the bigger-picture theory of change to all stakeholders and the community. The framework helps keep everyone on the same page and serves as a reminder of the bigger picture.

Palmer and Gross also noted that when developing the framework, they had to consider what they could control and what they could influence. They knew that systems work doesn't always solve all issues, so they needed to be realistic in thinking through what they could change and accomplish through this work. Palmer and Gross also had to think about the impact the programs and services could have and if the outcomes could be measured. It was important to them to make sure any evaluation was not too burdensome or costly and that it gave them information that was truly helpful and not just done for the sake of collecting data.

In addition, the framework helps build buy-in and acceptance. Palmer and Gross were mindful to capture the major strategies without excluding any significant component. The women added that although the framework may not reflect all partner services, it captures the main points of the work in a way that includes and reflects all involved.

For Palm Beach County, the framework continues to evolve as the county incorporates lessons learned from years of implementation and responds to changes in funding or political and societal contexts.

Children's Services Council Pathway to Early Childhood Development

Goals: What We Want			
CHILDREN ARE BORN HEALTHY	CHILDREN ARE SAFE FROM ABUSE AND NEGLECT	CHILDREN ARE READY FOR KINDERGARTEN	CHILDREN HAVE ACCESS TO QUALITY AFTERSCHOOL AND SUMMER PROGRAMS

Child Outcomes: What We Measure			
↓ rate of infant mortality, percent of premature births, and percent of low-birthweight births	↓ percent of children (birth to age five) with verified abuse or neglect	↑ percent of children scoring ready on the state kindergarten readiness assessment	↑ number of children enrolled in quality afterschool or summer programs

Key Indicators: What We Track		
↑ Expectant mothers receiving early and adequate prenatal care ↑ Expectant mothers who have health care coverage ↑ Mothers receiving interconception health care education ↑ Adult mothers with subsequent births at least 24 months apart ↓ Births among teens ↓ Subsequent teen births ↓ Expectant mothers and parents of young children with depression, trauma, stress, and mental health concerns	↑ Children who receive ongoing developmental surveillance ↑ Identification of young children who need early intervention service (social-emotional, behavioral, developmental, and disability) ↑ Parents and children who have positive and nurturing relationships ↑ Children with emergent literacy skills ↑ Parents/adults reading to their children ↑ Parents engaged in their children's learning	↑ Children in high-quality early care and education programs ↑ Children with social-emotional competence ↑ Children who have health care insurance ↑ Children who have a primary health care provider ↑ Children who receive age-appropriate immunizations and well-child visits within the recommended time period ↓ Children who experience summer learning loss

Primary Strategies: What We Do			
• Facilitate access to prenatal and interconception care • Promote child and maternal health and wellness • Engage teens in positive activities to prevent teen pregnancy	• Address maternal depression, trauma, toxic stress, and mental health concerns • Enhance parenting skills and knowledge of child development	• Address child developmental concerns • Promote physical, cognitive, social, and emotional competence and development among young children	• Promote family and early childhood literacy • Provide resources and supports that expand access to quality early care and education, and afterschool summer programs

CHAPTER 6

Putting Collaborative Leadership into Practice

NOW IT'S TIME to put all the ideas behind the systems-building planning process into action. You will need ways to bring planning participants together, have productive meetings, make decisions, and guide group members through the planning process. This chapter provides information on how to begin the group work, including determination of roles and responsibilities, meeting facilitation, communication strategies, and meeting structure. It also includes ideas for developing a shared purpose and vision as well as a clear process. I end the chapter with a section on dealing with conflict, as working through change will inevitably have rough patches.

Identify Members and Develop Roles and Responsibilities

Involving key team members in the planning process is important. And considering a diverse range of ideas, opinions, and viewpoints is imperative. Finally, including input and feedback from all levels of the collaborative work to ensure vertical and horizontal participation is critical. Members should not just be those in leadership positions or higher levels. Hearing from those up and down the vertical levels of participating organizations as well as horizontally across levels, sectors, organizations, and roles is crucial. Also strive to involve key stakeholders and partners who are critical to the work and to the success of the collaboration. Think of stakeholders and partners who should be involved. Some will be obvious, while others may not. Think of definitive stakeholders who should be in the room, and then think about who is not in the room. The following members must be involved in the planning process:

- those with decision-making power
- those affected or impacted by any decisions
- individuals or organizations with expertise, information, or ideas
- those who could block or impede decisions

Also important is determining and documenting collaborative member roles. This helps clarify responsibilities and empowers members to work toward common goals. It also makes it easier for new members to join and to keep the process transparent. The roles and members may change over time, depending on the nature and details of the projects. For example, funding may increase or decrease, goals may change, or the surrounding context or circumstances may change. Or perhaps new members may be added to the partnership as the need for more information increases.

Meeting Facilitation

In collaborative teamwork, there are many players and countless details to track. Building and maintaining a strong collaboration and an effective, transparent process requires paying attention to the details and working through them while steadily making progress. Leaders may have some of the skills required, but it could be necessary to bring in a facilitator to keep track of all the details and manage the process. Systems-building efforts take time and have many moving parts. Ensuring that progress is ongoing and that details and relationships are maintained as effectively as possible is critical.

Designate a Facilitator

A facilitator is sometimes key to a collaborative systems-building effort. Designating or bringing in a facilitator will provide structure to manage the process, maintain relationships, include diverse stakeholders, work effectively together toward a common vision, and incorporate all ideas, challenges, issues, and strengths. All involved must come to the table, determine how willing they are to work together, and build the relationships and trust required to stay at the table. This can be difficult work. Having a neutral party to guide the process can really help, as it allows those involved to fully participate, engage in the tough conversations, and work toward change. To let go of individual interests and shift toward working for the good of the whole requires the assurance that the process is safe enough to do so. A facilitator can help establish this sense of safety and create an environment and culture that supports innovation, creativity, collaboration, and change.

Functions of a Facilitator

The main function of a facilitator is to act as a neutral party to help assist the collaborative systems-building effort. To gain and maintain the trust needed to guide the meetings, a facilitator must come to the process without bias or personal interests or investments.

A facilitator has three main roles:

- **Guide the process.** A facilitator's main role is to guide the process, the meetings, and the conversations. This includes keeping the process clear, inclusive, respectful, and productive. Facilitators don't come up with the ideas, but they do set the agenda.
- **Describe and interpret the process.** A facilitator also demystifies the process and ensures that it remains transparent. He or she helps break down the process, describe it, and make sure that all know what is happening.
- **Provide methods and strategies.** A facilitator has a repertoire of strategies and ideas to keep meeting agendas productive, keep the process on task, and ensure continued progress. A facilitator prevents the group from getting stuck or lost in the process and has tools to maintain the structure and keep the process organized.

Importance of Physical Space

David Straus (2002, 140) notes the significance of the physical space in which meetings are held. Having meeting rooms set up in a way that fosters collaboration so "the focus will not be on one another or on the meeting leader, but on a common task" is important. Therefore, arriving at meetings early to set up the room in a way that supports collaboration is key. Straus recommends a semicircle as the best setup because it opens up the space yet focuses the energy of the group in a common direction while still allowing group members to make eye contact. The curve of the semicircle can convey teamwork and collaboration while enabling all in the group to see a facilitator, focus on neutral ground, and see each other.

Feeling relaxed and comfortable in meeting spaces is important because comfort facilitates collaboration. If the space feels too formal or as if the stakes are too high, then people will feel less inclined to share honestly and build trust. Rosen (2007, 57) says, "Informality enhances collaboration."

Goffin (2015) suggests including "homey touches," such as art and plants, to create an inviting environment to work in. One collaborative meeting I attend monthly always has some sort of table decorations or centerpieces—often plants, flowers, or something colorful or from nature. Decorations do create a happy and relaxed atmosphere in which to have a meeting.

In addition to comfortable seating and inviting décor, provide items to obtain a record of the process and to capture the ideas that are agreed upon and the decisions that are made. All group members need to trust that their ideas are heard and have value. Sometimes paper and pens, flip charts, or whiteboards will be best to create an environment to freely brainstorm. Meetings may also feel more collaborative and more informal if there are ways to capture ideas in impermanent ways. For example, Rosen adds that sometimes the appeal of scribbling ideas on a napkin works well because it feels so temporary and therefore safer. Like a piece of paper, it can be crumpled up and thrown away. This can be more conducive to brainstorming because it creates the safety for group members to pitch ideas. Other times, it will be necessary to have the technology to create a more permanent record of the group's process and ideas. Therefore, be sure to provide materials and an environment that instills a sense of informality, collaboration, and brainstorming while also building a sense of trust in the process and safeguarding the group's ideas.

Establishing Communication Systems

If there is one thing I have learned through my years of leadership, it is that communication can make or break collaborations and systems-building efforts. Misunderstandings or a lack of communication can hurt relationships and lead to lost information and a loss of trust. Communication must flow well to keep progress moving forward and to ensure a transparent and trusting process. If people don't know or understand what is happening, the process may start to shut down. Leaders with strong communication skills who pay close attention to what others are trying to communicate are critical to the success of any collaboration.

Developing a Communication Plan

One strategy is to come up with a plan of how communication will be maintained between the various partners and across the system. Developing a communication plan that maps out how information will flow can help everyone stay informed. A communication plan can also decrease information gaps and reduce confusion. It keeps the ownership and responsibility on the group and allows for ongoing collaboration, input, reflection, and strategizing. It also helps build and maintain trust by working to ensure that all members are included and stay informed.

Communication plans should map out the who, when, and how of information sharing across all levels of your systems-building efforts, while also taking into account both internal and external stakeholders and partners. The communication plan can include what will be communicated in person at meetings and what will be transmitted via email, phone calls, written documents such as notes or minutes, or other methods.

- **Internal**—Think about how communication will flow between the internal partners on the project. How and when will internal partners receive communication? Will you have a lead contact for each partner organization or entity? Or will there be a lead for each component or topic area of the project? Each partner entity will also have to map out efficient communication channels to send information to those who need to know it within the organization. If there is a lead contact, that person will need to ensure that information gets to those who will be affected or who may need to follow up.
- **External**—How will everyone keep external partners and stakeholders informed? Will there be a lead agency to spearhead these efforts, or will all be responsible for this piece? How often will communication occur and in what form? Will you use newsletters, email blasts, social media posts, or press releases? How will you ensure a consistent, clear, and transparent message?
- **Across levels**—Make sure information adequately flows across all levels of the systems-building efforts. Information about what is being considered or decided needs to reach more than just those at the leadership levels—it needs to flow across all levels of the organizations and the system itself. People at all levels need access to information and opportunities to provide input and ideas. Those most affected by what is being discussed and decided often have the best ideas about what works, possible challenges and barriers, and the most effective solutions and opportunities.

Conversations with Intent

As part of the communication plan, some organizations strategize how the conversations will be structured. It is important for everyone to have information, but effective communication is also key, as it leads toward intended goals and provides opportunities to explore ideas. Goffin writes of convening conversations with intent, or that can be framed, structured, or customized to address current circumstances or needs. Goffin (2015, 62) states, "The design of conversations with intent should reflect their purpose." The goal is to be intentional about communication and what will be discussed, yet open enough to allow for new ideas or impromptu brainstorming sessions. Goffin also suggests structuring the conversations by asking specific questions and then allowing enough time for conversation. Plan for about twenty to thirty minutes for each guiding question.

Thinking about the physical structure of the conversations may also be helpful. If the conversation includes many people, then arranging everyone into groups of four to five people will enable all to participate and have a chance to be heard. Have people face each other, perhaps in a circle or across a table, so all feel included and able to engage with each other.

Beginning and Closing Conversations

Effective communication and conversations often have a planned beginning and end. When conducting an in-person meeting, allow enough time for people to mingle, check in, and get settled. This creates a positive and relaxed atmosphere before diving into the specific topic of discussion. For both in-person and written communication, include an introduction to the topic or questions, perhaps giving any background or history about how the work has evolved to this point. Providing such background information helps all feel included in the process, acknowledges the work and effort that have already occurred, and allows for all to begin the next stage of communication from the same point.

Also give some thought as to how and where the conversation will end. As Goffin (2015, 68) reminds us, "Giving consideration to the conversation's closure is as important as attending to the conversation's start." It helps to have time to summarize what was written or discussed, wrap up the conversation, talk about what remains to be worked on, and document any next steps. This builds trust, fosters responsibility and accountability, ensures a transparent process, and identifies who will work on each next step and how others might provide input or participate.

Meeting Process

Every step of the process is an opportunity to provide leadership and set the tone. How the meetings are planned, run, and documented can dramatically influence the collaborative efforts. A leader or facilitator's role is often to maintain and safeguard the process and the information. Establishing the tone and any procedures from the outset maximizes the likelihood of a successful collaboration.

Ground Rules

Setting ground rules establishes the structure for the meetings themselves. Going through this process together as a collaborative exercise helps create ownership and accountability for the group. People are more likely to feel positive and abide by the protocols if they helped set the rules themselves. As the facilitator, come to the first meeting with a few ground rules in mind to help get the ideas flowing. Rules that ensure a safe, trusting, and inclusive process are a good starting point.

Working together as leaders to set ground rules provides an opportunity to champion key values such as respect, inclusion, trust, and equity. This is a perfect time to begin to lay the foundation and set the tone for how the group will function, how the meetings will unfold, and how the collaborative process will happen.

Agendas and Minutes

With prepared agendas and a plan to document discussions and decisions, a transparent and inclusive process can take shape. An agenda helps all involved parties know what will be happening in the meeting, while minutes provide a record of what took place and what was decided. Agendas also provide a road map of topics, establishing a meeting that works for all involved, giving everyone ways to participate, and providing opportunities to work toward goals. Following are some key items to keep in mind when preparing agendas:

- **Set clear meeting goals.** Establish and state clear meeting goals at the top of each agenda or at the beginning of each meeting. This ensures the agenda is structured to meet the goals and keep the discussions focused.
- **Begin meetings with a simple check-in.** Build relationships and set the tone for inclusive team building by including a structured activity or allowing time for people to check in. Some social time prior to the start of the meeting or an icebreaker activity provides opportunities for people to form connections while jump-starting hearts and minds for the work ahead.
- **Set up opportunities to build trust.** Include ways to build trust through the activities set forth in the agenda. Working in small groups can help build trust among group members, as can solving a problem together or making a decision. Structuring ways for group members to safely take risks or voice ideas or opinions can also enhance trust.

- **Take risks as a leader.** One thing I keep in mind as a leader is that if I ask group members to take a risk, then I must be willing to do so as well. If an activity is to share an idea, contribute a solution, share a personal story, or make a new suggestion, then I must be willing to do so too. This can be a tricky balance, as you don't want to dominate the meeting or make it about you. But the group has to see that you are also willing to put yourself out there with them.
- **Use stories, quotes, or anecdotes.** Remembering that the work you are embarking on will have real impact or lead to tangible outcomes is beneficial. Hearing stories from the population you serve or from the group members themselves can be inspiring. It helps remind the group of the purpose and goals of the work and can motivate everyone to bring their best selves to the work ahead.
- **Review accomplishments.** Acknowledge contributions and work that was accomplished. Also review what happened and what didn't get done. Determine follow-up activities and action items for in between meetings and set agenda items for the next meeting.

Decision-Making Process

There will be many decisions to make and countless things to consider in a collaboration, so it is critical to establish a decision-making process early on. Without a plan for making decisions, the collaborative process may be slowed down or could end up in confusion and chaos. You will need a way to clearly make decisions in order to make progress toward goals.

Decision-making can be approached in a variety of ways, but the process should be transparent and information should be accessible to all involved. Systems-building work may affect various people, organizations, and services, so it's important for all to know how decisions are made and what the decisions are. The best way to ensure that all are supportive of decisions and committed to upholding them is to work to make sure all agree on the decision-making processes and models the group will use. Getting everyone to agree can take time, but it will be worthwhile in the long run. There will be more buy-in and support, and better long-term outcomes if all agree on the decision-making processes.

There are many different decision-making models to choose from. Below is a list of some of the more generally agreed-upon processes for decision-making (Roberts 2010):

- **Input**—The group gives input and ideas, which will be factored into a subsequent decision to be made by another individual or group.

- **Recommendations**—The group reaches an agreement or decision that will then be sent on to the decision-making individual or group to finalize or reject.
- **Majority**—When using a majority model, the agreed-upon decision receives at least 50 percent of the votes cast.
- **Supermajority**—This model requires support from a majority greater than 50 percent (such as two-thirds or three-fifths) to make a decision.
- **Consensus**—The whole group supports the decision. This does not mean that everyone completely agrees, but instead that all have participated, contributed opinions, and feel as if they can live with and actively support the decision.

Determining which decision-making model to use depends on many factors, including the context and the details of the decisions and process. Below are aspects to consider as you determine which decision-making model to use:

- **Time**—How much time is there to make the decision?
- **Importance**—How important is this decision?
- **Buy-in**—How much buy-in is there among the stakeholders and decision makers?
- **Information**—Do the decision makers have all the information they need? Is more information or expertise needed?
- **Strategic opportunities**—What opportunities does this decision create or impact?

The more time allowed for the process, the more freedom team members have to work collectively through decision-making. And if the decisions are significant and require substantial buy-in, then all involved stakeholders need to be part of the decision-making process. The group will need to decide which are the best options, given the parameters and goals of the group. Often in collaborative efforts, groups strive to make decisions by consensus so that all involved come to a unanimously supported decision.

Building Consensus

Consensus is when there is unanimous support for the decision. It means the group reaches a decision that each member agrees to support. Each person agrees it is the best decision and can actively support it, even if it may not have been his or her top choice. It does not mean that anyone has had to compromise his or her interests or jeopardize what he or she feels is right. If any one person cannot buy into the decision, then there is not consensus.

Building consensus is often obtainable but sometimes hard to reach. It takes time and a high level of commitment. But achieving consensus is worth the effort. It leads to high-quality decisions as it connects what is possible with what is right. Building consensus must factor in the ideas, opinions, and values of all involved, but it also asks members to put the collective vision and goals ahead of their personal beliefs or desires. If consensus is reached, it often involves a synergy of the group coming together in support of the decision.

Building consensus often involves going through steps of defining, analyzing, and deciding on the issues. Straus (2002) suggests there are six phases involved in building consensus:

1. **Perception**—Is there a problem? How does each person feel about it?
2. **Definition**—What is the problem? How would we define it? What are its limits or parameters?
3. **Analysis**—What are the causes of the problem? Why is it a problem?
4. **Determine solutions**—What are some solutions to the problem? What are some other alternatives?
5. **Evaluation**—What criteria does the best solution need to meet? Which alternatives are the best or better than the others?
6. **Decision making**—Which solution can the group agree on? Which decision can each member actively support and commit to?

Consensus building may not always be a perfect, linear process. There will, at times, be some jumping back and forth between phases. The group may have to step back to better define the problem or may determine alternative solutions that may not have been thought of before. New sources of information may provide further analysis of the problem or add additional evaluation criteria. Some of this may be beneficial, and some may begin to impede the process. As a group you may need to have a process by which you decide to move through each phase or agree to go back and revisit other ideas. For consensus building to work, the group must move through each phase together and remain focused on the same phase at the same time.

Although a facilitator needs to keep the consensus-building process moving forward, it may sometimes help to remind the group that they can go back if they need to build agreement for the current phase. Another option is to ask if everyone can live with this definition of the problem or if everyone is ready to move on to solutions. Building in agreement in small increments, conditions for ideas, and trade-off will help move the process forward.

However, consensus may not always be possible. It is best to determine a fallback or alternative decision-making process in the event consensus is not reached. This is best done early on, when determining decision-making processes, instead of waiting until disagreement happens. Having a plan in place keeps the process positive and the group focused on the decisions rather than the ability to agree or not. Then the group knows in advance that if consensus isn't reached, they will go with decision-making strategy number two, a plan the group is already familiar with.

Process Mapping

Although sometimes you may need to design the process as you go, most of the time it is best to develop a process and process map to guide and articulate the course of the work. There is no one way to do this, as each systems-building effort is unique. Each process has different goals, stakeholders, challenges, constraints, timelines, and participants. But it is possible to develop a process in advance to guide the work. A process map lays out the plan of how the group intends to proceed and helps the group navigate its own path.

Including the group and stakeholders in the development of the process map is important. It won't work to try to impose a process that the group didn't design and doesn't buy into. For people to invest in and trust the process, they need to be part of creating it. This also helps everyone step back and see the big picture and the goals. It helps everyone see the complexities involved and the time it might take, and discern the best approach. These things will help determine the sequence of steps, the priorities, and the order in which they need to be tackled. Working through this process together establishes a trust between members that allows the group to be more flexible when new ideas or issues arise.

Visually, a process may take on any number of forms. It could be a diagram, table, or chart. It could look more like a game board or road map. It may involve shapes and arrows. The key is to capture the process in a way that works for the group, is transparent, and demonstrates to all stakeholders how they have agreed to proceed and how they will be involved.

Although process maps may take on different looks, they will likely contain some of the same phases or steps (Straus 2002):

- **Education or learning phase**—bringing all members of the group up to date on the issues
- **Visioning phase**—reaching an agreement about what it could look like if the issue or problem were solved
- **Information phase**—gathering data, facts, and information about the current situation

- **Definition and analysis phase**—determining the issues and problems, defining them, and understanding the underlying causes
- **Solutions phase**—generating alternative solutions to the problems
- **Evaluation and test phase**—testing out the possible solutions and evaluating the effectiveness
- **Decision phase**—making final decisions based on the best scenarios, solutions, plans, and systems plan

Fostering Collaborative Group Process

It will be important throughout the process to foster the group members' collaborative work with one another. For all involved to remain dedicated to the work requires participants to maintain a commitment to the same purpose, vision, and end goals. Taking the time early on in the process to establish this commitment, and having strategies to sustain this collaborative group process throughout the planning stage, is advantageous.

Developing a Shared Purpose and Vision

A shared purpose and vision is essential to building trust and ensuring progress. Without a shared agreement about the reasons to work together and a cohesive vision of the team's direction, making progress will be difficult. All members of the group have to agree on and believe in the purpose. And to successfully reach goals, the group needs to begin with a vision of the ideal end goal.

Create a Vision Statement

Envision how you want your system to look when you reach your goal. What would success look like? The vision statement should capture the beliefs of the group and become the focal point for the work. It's the cohesive bond that holds the group to the work and brings the members together. The vision statement is focused on the optimistic possibilities of the future. It holds out for what could be without worrying about how to get there or the problems the group might face along the way.

A vision statement should include the following information:

- **What will be accomplished**—What will be the result of the work?
- **The scope of what will be accomplished**—Who will benefit from the work, and how much of an impact will there be?
- **The unique purpose of the work**—How is this work unique or different from what has been done before?

To begin the work, brainstorm words or phrases. Come up with a list of critical words or ideas that are part of the vision. Then, through discussion, activities, and decisions, work to whittle down and agree on the most important ideas or the ones that have the most consensus in the group. This whole process may take time, but it will be well worth the time invested. A clear vision statement will inspire and motivate the group toward the desired end results. It will guide the steps of the process, the decision points, and the actions necessary to fulfill the vision.

Harnessing Group Memory

The group memory is the record of all the ideas contributed and decisions made by the group. It is the visual display and documentation of the group's process, including challenges, solutions, problems solved, and all input and decisions. More than just note taking, group memory is a way to both foster and verify the group process, value all viewpoints, and honor all decisions.

Be sure to record the group memory in a way that all can see. Individual notes may represent only one view or interpretation and are often not available to all until after the meeting. To the contrary, by writing down ideas on chart paper up on a wall or easel, you are developing a visual tracking system of all ideas and decisions. Recording the group work visually can help the collaborative process in significant ways. Doing so can increase group focus and recollection, increase understanding of agreements, level the playing field, decrease repetition, and help integrate new members.

Increase group focus and recollection. I have been in meetings where I can't recall where we left off or what we focused on in the last meeting. Having a running record and going over it at the start of each new meeting can help the group focus on the process. Recounting what happened in the past serves as an introduction to the current meeting, helping the group concentrate on the agenda and the tasks at hand. Rather than flipping sheets of paper over the back of the easel, it may help to tape completed sheets around the room to better foster and honor group memory. This way everyone can see the group process and take in all the ideas and decisions that have been recorded.

Increase understanding of agreements. Sometimes people leave a meeting with different interpretations or understandings of what took place and what was agreed on. Charting the group process and group decisions in front of all group members is a powerful facilitative strategy to increase group understanding on all decisions and agreements. It opens up dialogue about what is written and encourages discussion of each point to clarify information and come into agreement about meaning.

Level the playing field. Often in meetings, group members come with different levels of authority and status as well as varying degrees of expertise and information. Capturing all group members' ideas without assigning priority, judgment, or opinion can help level the playing field. In addition, it passes ownership of the ideas to the whole group rather than to only a handful of people. As Straus (2002, 134) notes, "The recorder does not and should not serve as gatekeeper for ideas." Instead, all ideas should be written down so that everyone can see and value all contributions and give them equal consideration. This will create safety and trust in the group process, provide a balance of power, and foster a collaborative process.

Decrease repetition. Repetition can be a common problem in meetings and with group processes. Not only is it frustrating, but getting stuck in a spinning cycle of repetition can inhibit progress. For a collaborative process to stay healthy and continue to engage members, its members must effectively record, value, and use group memory to avoid repetition.

Integrate new members. If there is documented history, then it becomes easier for new members to catch up. Systems-building efforts can be lengthy, and the players may change. Members new to the process may have missed much of what happened before. This can be a good thing, as new members will come with fresh ideas and new perspectives—especially if they can easily get caught up on the process and quickly learn about decisions that have already been made.

The Role of Conflict

Collaboration and systems building will bring together a wealth of knowledge from diverse stakeholders. These processes may also bring together different sectors, such as nonprofit with the business sector or a government body. Funding may also be inadequate or come and go. All this can, and will, lead to challenges, differing opinions, and conflicts. These things are part of the work. Change can be hard, and sometimes conflict feels difficult or scary, especially in a field that values relationships, positive interactions, and happy and healthy children and families. But conflict is an essential aspect of the work, and as leaders, we need to expect it, plan for it, and learn to welcome and embrace it.

Expect and Plan for Conflict

Conflict is inevitable when working to do things differently than they are done today. And that is okay. Conflict can be a good thing, as it will lead to new ideas and new opportunities. The key is to expect conflict, plan for it, and change your perspective about it. We often view conflict as something negative. But it is possible, and even necessary, for leaders to have a positive view or attitude toward conflict. Janet Gonzalez-Mena (2013, 1) describes the idea of "dancing with conflict." She writes, "Thinking of an argument like a dance changes the image. And changing the image gives you power!" Perceiving conflict as a partnership, or an exchange of ideas without anyone being right or wrong, and without winners or losers, is a powerful approach.

Sullivan (2016, 10) adds, "Conflict and disagreement are perfect opportunities to learn something new, something different." She states that to dance with conflict, one has to both view conflict as a good thing and be open to diversity. "Diversity can work only if we make room for one more idea, one more belief, one more perspective, one more practice, one more value. Then we can begin the dance with conflict." Again, this reinforces the idea that conflict can be a good thing, because it can open up new ideas and new possibilities.

Chris Amirault (pers. comm.) talks of "structuring tensions" as a way to plan for and acknowledge conflict. To structure tensions means to switch attention to conflict and embrace problems because they can be empowering. "Conflicts are exactly the place to invest power," Amirault suggests, because they help you work through the things that need attention or resolution, or to be acknowledged. Unintended consequences and imperfections are okay. Having leaders who have developed a tolerance for problems and conflict and are able to persist through them is critical.

Keep in mind that not all problems are going to be solved. Systems aren't perfect. Especially in a field without adequate funding or policies or political will, not everything can be solved with one collaboration or one systems-building effort. Often we will have to balance equity with quality or culture with standards. Systems will not make all the problems go away, and when embarking on this work, we don't have to try to make it perfect. "All these imperfections are your friend," says Amirault, because they help you focus power and attention, be open to diverse ideas, include all views, and, as Gonzalez-Mena and Sullivan might say, be open to the dance.

Conflict Resolution Strategies and Solutions

Conflicts can be challenging but are often resolvable. Although resolving conflicts may take time, resources, and a lot of patience, solutions often can be determined. You may not be able to solve everything, and most certainly not in ways that are perfect for all involved. But frequently ways to work through conflicts that address the issues at hand can be found.

Create a Conflict Resolution Process

Having the facilitation and the decision-making process already established will be helpful. You can use both of these key pieces to help determine your approach to working through conflicts. Find a facilitator for the process to help maintain trust and stick to agreed-upon values and decision-making structures, and to stay true to the greater vision and goals. The facilitator and all involved can also work together to determine and agree about how best to make decisions regarding the conflict.

Winer and Ray (1994, 79) also suggest that the process must "separate the conflict from concepts of right and wrong." This helps keep the focus on the issues and avoids making it personal. Sometimes conflicts come to be associated with the people involved or their ideas or beliefs. Focusing on the issue, not right or wrong ideas or individual beliefs, will keep the process on track toward the bigger vision while maintaining trust and including all viewpoints.

It is also important to make sure everyone is heard. Winer and Ray say the process should include ways to rein in those who talk a lot and to encourage the participation of those who speak less often. Ideas and solutions can often come from those who have been less directly involved or those more removed who are able to see the issues from a different perspective than those in the heart of it. Allowing for all voices to be heard also ensures that all involved have a way to contribute and that the process and the resolution belong to the whole group. It empowers a collective process and helps build a trusting collaboration.

Clarify the Issues

The first step is to clarify and name the issues. Often people see the issues in different ways, or they have a different understanding of what they perceive the conflict to be. Clarifying and naming the issues can help clear up misunderstandings or misinformation and can begin to address the conflict itself.

Think about when we work with children to solve problems. A first step is often to ask, "What's happening?" and give each child an opportunity to explain things from her or his perspective. Then the teachers can help clarify the problem (for example, establishing that the problem is that both children want the same truck—not that one child is a dummy and can't come to the other child's birthday party and that the other child had the truck first). This same process is effective when working collaboratively with adults.

In clarifying the issue, striving to understand the cause, if there is one, is also helpful. The likelihood of solving the problem increases if the underlying factor or source of the issue is known and understood. Below are some typical sources of conflict:

Unclear vision or mission. Unclear vision or lack of agreement on the best approaches toward meeting goals can lead to confusion and conflict. If people have different ideas about where they thought their effort was focused, conflicts will arise and group members may need to rethink their positions and their investment in the process.

Power struggles. Egos or the need for power sometimes can be at the root of a conflict or can disrupt the collaborative process. Often this can also be about fear of losing control, identity, a competitive advantage, and/or resources. There can be real stakes in these systems-building endeavors, and sometimes emotions and tensions can rise among group members as they grapple with tough issues and negotiate for their own interests.

Lack of trust or confidence. If group members feel a lack of trust and/or confidence in the process or in other group members or entities, this will result in conflict at some point. These may be long-standing conflicts and may reside under the surface.

- **Harboring the elephants**—When elephants in the room remain unnamed, conflict can ensue, inhibiting true progress.
- **Lack of transparency**—If group members feel a lack of trust, they may hold back on giving input or providing information.
- **Hidden agendas**—All involved need to have the greater good in mind and align with the agreed-upon mission and vision. Alternative hidden agendas will erode trust and lead to conflict.

Systemic issues. Some things may be very difficult to achieve or resolve because of the systemic issues in play that interfere with the work. Political and/or governance structures, lack of infrastructure, inefficient data systems, or regulation and policy limitations or restrictions can greatly impede progress and result in tough choices for the group to work through.

Lack of resources. A lack of resources is a source of conflict, for it can often force the group to make difficult decisions. The group members may have to compromise on hoped-for goals or outcomes if they lack the resources to meet them. Conflicts can arise as all work together to set priorities and determine allocation of resources to best meet the purpose.

Strengthen Vision, Trust, and Relationships

Go back to the basics of why the group came together. Revisit the vision statements and revise or recommit if needed. Do some team-building and trust-strengthening activities and find ways to resolve the unvoiced tensions or elephants in the room. People should be honest about why they are there and if the work still fits with their agenda and ability to participate and contribute. This is difficult but critical to the work. Everyone has to be in the process together and maintain strong relationships and trust; otherwise conflicts will continue to surface.

Generate Solutions

Solutions and ways to resolve challenging issues can almost always be found. Conflict helps us look at the hard stuff and find a way through it, around it, or over it. It shows us where we need to focus attention and make changes. In the end, the group process is often stronger and better for having faced the challenges and tackled the hard decisions needed to improve the work. Below are some helpful tips to keep in mind when working to generate solutions:

Solutions are out there. Maintain an optimistic attitude, because solutions are out there, especially if you are open to them. And you never know where a good idea might come from. Ask all involved, including stakeholders, for solutions. Often those working closely with an issue have ideas to solve it. And sometimes those close to an issue can't see a solution, but those looking in from a different vantage point can. So cast a wide net and see what ideas come up.

Allow time for solutions. Most things do not have to be solved immediately. Taking time to look at the issues from various perspectives and hearing diverse opinions usually helps. Potential solutions sometimes have to be thought out, tested, and mulled over before landing on the best one. Some solutions need to be dissected in order to even understand all the various issues or components. Taking the time to hear from others and learn about all aspects of the conflict can allow things that may not have otherwise come up to be voiced, reflected on, and figured out.

Solutions can transcend positions. Conflict doesn't have to be locked into opposing sides or positions of an issue. Conflict is also not about right and wrong. Gonzalez-Mena (2013, 3) writes of the "third space perspective," which begins with realizing there can be another perspective beyond the obvious two sides of an issue. She encourages viewing the conflict through that lens instead. For this approach to work, both parties must be willing to step out of their positions and see the issue from another vantage point. It's not compromise or even meeting halfway but coming at the issue in an entirely different way. Gonzalez-Mena gives the analogy of blue and yellow coming together to form green, a whole new color. To view conflict this way requires respect. It also requires really listening to the other party and striving to understand his or her viewpoint, values, and goals.

Include everyone. Make sure everyone is heard and has a voice in the process. This may mean working to limit those who speak often and encouraging those who do not speak often. Conflicts can bring up power and control issues. Empowering all not only helps generate more solutions and ideas but builds trust and relationships and ensures an inclusive process. The solutions will also be more successful if all feel as if they were included in solving the problem and reached a consensus on the resolution.

Not everything needs to be solved. The group may have to let some things go, especially conflicts that arise from bigger, systemic issues. Although they may not be perfect, solutions that best address issues can be agreed on, even when resources are limited. Document and keep track of solutions and those issues that couldn't be resolved with current resources, time, or circumstances. The group can always work with policymakers, funders, or others to make these parties aware of the issues and address the problem areas. In this underresourced and frequently devalued field, later solutions can and will happen. We need to remain focused on building what we can and creating the best systems within current realities. Amazing work can be done and great things can be created. Focusing on that and not getting bogged down or discouraged by what can't be solved now helps everyone maintain a positive attitude.

Working through Conflict: Structuring Tensions

Oregon has been working to revise the state's early childhood education quality rating and improvement systems (QRIS). The state worked with a consultant to facilitate and guide the process. Together they created vision statements describing the key values of the revised QRIS. The statements include "Ensure inclusion of diversity of cultures, communities of color, ethnicities, languages and abilities using the Oregon Equity Lens; Be efficient, effective, and build upon existing systems;" and "Be understood and valued by all stakeholders" (Oregon Department of Education, 2016). They also developed guiding principles as a commitment to the revision process itself. These principles will help the group ensure that the process will "be transparent and inclusive; recognize and value all stakeholders; be data driven and vision focused;" and "explicitly focus on equity and reflecting diversity of cultures, communities of color, ethnicities, languages and abilities." They also deliberately discussed and documented what they call the "tension points" as a way to uncover and talk about the conflicts and problems. Documenting these tension points was a strategy to give voice to them and to publicly say that the issues were recognized and needed attention, even if they could not be resolved. Chris Amirault (pers. comm.), the consultant who supported the process, states that the tension points are written to show the balance of the two sides of issues so as "to see the bigger picture of all the elements, not to change minds, but to develop a tolerance for the problems and conflict and persist through it." Tension points include: the "importance of high quality early childhood experiences *and* the subjective nature of 'quality'; inclusion of all children *and* priority of children furthest from opportunity; scope of involvement of licensed programs *and* increasing focus on full continuum of care; goal of school readiness *and* importance of the whole child;" and the "desire to provide information to/educate families and partner with them as experts and decision makers" (Oregon Department of Education 2016). Acknowledging and structuring these tensions provides a way to both give voice to them and own the inherent conflicts within them. Acknowledgment elevates conflicts in the priority queue, marking them as issues to continue to work through without getting stuck. It helps determine where and how power is invested in the tensions while moving ahead with systems-building work.

CHAPTER 7

Leadership for Multidimensional Systems Change

GOVERNANCE, AUTHORITY, and accountability are necessary for providing sustained leadership of changed systems. Understanding how this new multidimensional system will operate and have ongoing governance structures in place and operationalized authority to make decisions is critical to implementing and sustaining the work. This chapter will provide information and ideas on authority and accountability and discuss different possibilities within and across multiple agencies and sectors. It will also include thoughts on how to be accountable in authentic ways so as to reduce barriers and inequities in the system. And finally, this chapter will explore how to build leadership teams and address issues of power to support ongoing collaboration.

Understanding and Defining Governance Structures

Establishing governance structures is a crucial infrastructure component of systems-building work. The main function of the governance structure is to establish authority and ensure accountability. A governance structure is what will enable the system to operate effectively. In short, a system needs to have in place a way to govern itself. Kagan and Kauerz (2012, 88) define governance as "the structure, processes, and policies that enable a system to function consistently, effectively, and efficiently." The purpose of governance is to implement, maintain, oversee, and administer the system framework. In some ways, it is the glue that holds the system together and gives the system the power to operate.

Authority

There should be an agreed-upon body or entity with the authority to effectively make decisions and establish and maintain policies. Ideally, this body or structure should be representative of the larger system and have the support needed to be credible and influential. A system can fail if there is insufficient power or authority to create and implement policies or take action and make decisions that matter and can have impact.

Here are some responsibilities the governance structure may include:

- develop and implement policies and regulations
- address and reduce barriers
- establish criteria, guidelines, standards, qualifications, or competencies
- determine services and programs
- manage finances, budgets, and fiscal resources
- define data, evaluation needs, and processes

Accountability

Governance should include the structures that enable the system to be accountable to the various stakeholders. The governance body must develop the means to collect and analyze data and information about how the system is working, if outcomes are being met, and if the programs and services are reaching people and addressing issues effectively. Furthermore, the governing body must relay this information to those involved in the system and those affected by it. To be truly accountable, methods must be in place for maintaining accountability and disseminating this information.

Below is a list of items the governance needs to be accountable for:

- finances to ensure money is being spent appropriately
- delivery and accessibility of services
- program quality and effectiveness

Intra-agency

Within a single agency, governance structures need to provide for collaborative cross-department work to think and function systemically. Sometimes, even within a single agency, one department doesn't know what the others are doing and therefore can't function systemically as part of a whole. For effective collaboration to take place across departments, structural changes may need to be made. For example, a single agency could establish cross-department head governance teams with staff-level work groups to conduct systems work across the agency. Or perhaps an organization could create a department that is specifically focused on intra-agency functions and cross-department integration and alignment.

Cross-Agency

Establishing a systems approach across agencies within the same sector will require establishing a governance structure for the cross-agency work. With similar missions, populations served, and possibly services or approaches, this work will have its challenges and opportunities. Each agency will have its own independent culture, financial structures, fiscal constraints or possibilities, service areas, personnel needs, workforce policies, and qualifications, in addition to its own governance and accountability. All of this must be factored into how the cross-agency governance will be established.

For cross-agency governance, an entity such as a council, advisory board, leadership team, or some type of commission may need to be established. Standards for authority and accountability will need to be developed, approved, and adopted by the governing body and accepted by each participating agency. This is an important step in establishing the governing body as the legitimate authority. Each partner agency must support and honor the authority of the cross-agency governing entity.

Depending on the nature of the work, formal agreements of some type may need to be developed. Exactly what is needed will depend on the level of authority and financial structures of the systems work. If the governing entity is more a collaborative body with an advisory role, then something less formal may suffice. Also, if there are no financial connections or oversight, then a Memorandum of Understanding (MOU) may be sufficient. If the relationship between agencies involves finances, a decision-making authority, or shared programmatic standards of operating, then formal contracts will be needed to spell out the specific terms of each relationship.

An Innovative Countywide Approach

One highly effective collaboration system with cross-agency governance is an alliance of ten organizations serving children and families across Los Angeles County. After working together over many years, the agencies decided to formally align their joint activities and fund a central coordinating office, the Child Care Alliance of Los Angeles (CCALA), which launched in 1997. Together, with this new structure, they were able to collaboratively negotiate and implement a large county child care subsidy contract and coordinate countywide activities. Through membership dues and grant funding, the CCALA is staffed with an executive director and multiple staff to coordinate various countywide projects. The governance structure is multileveled and includes a board made up of the top executives from each agency, three director/manager-level committees, as well as several subcommittees and work groups that meet monthly to coordinate and implement all joint projects and services. With distinct service areas reaching every corner of the county, the CCALA collectively provides child care subsidies to more than 46,500 children in more than 19,700 child care settings every month. Leveraging its collective impact, the alliance developed a comprehensive professional development system offering coordinated training, coaching, technical assistance, and support to child care providers across the county. CCALA provided 3,312 training workshops to 10,200 child care providers and supportive coaching to more than 3,000 providers between 2011 and 2016.

Within Government

If the authority resides within government, then the funding, lines of power, and standards may be clearer, or at least live within the government structures. How funds are allocated, how standards are maintained, and how data is collected is generally established by the authority of the government itself. There may be an advisory group made up of both governmental and nongovernmental personnel, but generally the leadership authority lies with a department of the government. And most states and counties have established systems for accountability, including regulations and policies. But federal, state, and other local government structures tend to be complex. Funding, standards, regulations, and programs often exist across multiple departments and divisions of government. Ideally, systems-building efforts would simplify or streamline efforts.

Cross-Sector

Working across multiple agencies requires a governance structure to manage the details of cross-agency work and the added complexities of multiple types of agencies with varying programs and services. Partner organizations will need to determine a way to share accountability and assume governance together. In addition to a shared vision, purpose, and goals, these collaborative systems will also need to develop budgets, financial structures, and shared standards regarding evaluation and data. The success of the program becomes a shared responsibility, and a governance group will need to be structured in such a way as to accomplish and maintain the system.

A Cross-Sector Approach to Improving Outcomes for Children

In South Los Angeles, community organizations came together to focus on the issues facing children and families in a high-need area of the county. The partnership "is a collaborative effort of eight health and human services organizations that partner to provide cross-agency care coordination for children from birth to age 5 in Los Angeles" (Partners for Children South L.A., accessed 2017). With a mission of improving developmental outcomes for children and reducing their involvement with the child welfare system, the partnership includes the following organizations:

- **Legal services**—Alliance for Children's Rights and the Legal Aid Foundation of Los Angeles
- **Early intervention and social services**—Children's Institute, Inc.; South Central Los Angeles Regional Center; Early Childhood Special Education Department—Los Angeles Unified School District; and the Service Planning Area (SPA) 6 Family Solution Center
- **Housing**—People Assisting the Homeless (PATH), Weingart Center for the Homeless, and Imagine LA
- **ECE access and services**—Crystal Stairs, Inc.; and Para Los Niños
- **Health care**—St. John's Well Child & Family Center
- **Employment**—South LA WorkSource Center
- **Foster youth**—First Place for Youth
- **Parenting support**—Girls Club of Los Angeles
- **Community engagement and development**—Community Coalition and the Institute for Maximum Human Potential

Collectively, these organizations have a system of care model that includes services beginning with intake and assessment through developing care plans and providing case management and referrals. Through this process, they are able to provide not only effective services but also links to other organizations and services in a coordinated, client-centered way. Together the partnership provides support groups, as well as referrals and connections to early interventions services, housing, legal assistance, child care, health care, mental health counseling, and more.

According to the director of the partnership, Liza Bray, this collaboration was initiated by funders who realized they were funding the same organizations and wanted to better leverage resources to improve their reach and outcomes. These funders brought organizations together and hired a consultant to help the group put territorial issues to the side and deconstruct the silos in which they had been operating. By leaving politics at the door and building partnerships and relationships, the funders achieved this collective impact model. Bray (pers. comm.) added that the success was in "bringing to the table those who believe in the power of collaboration at all levels of the organization."

• • • • • • • • • • • • • • •

Authentic Accountability

In systems building, those in higher-level leadership positions often make the decisions. Those at the staff level, who are the ones affected and actually implementing the programs, are not usually given the power to make decisions. As a result, accountability may not be aligned with how the work is really carried out. When this is the case, the system may actually perpetuate inequities, because the right strategies and activities are not being measured or the established standards can't possibly be achieved.

In addition, the ECE field historically has been one of fragmented governance and funding. This has led to inconsistent or unaligned standards and governance. Furthermore, the entire ECE field and related fields are usually underfunded. Within the confines of working in an underfunded field, we have to be aware of what we can and can't accomplish, as well as the underlying stress that affects those working within it. Our systems work must acknowledge and address these underlying issues and strive to reduce barriers and inequities.

When developing systems, we must be mindful about reframing accountability to eliminate the inequities and move the field forward. Authentic accountability involves making sure we are asking the right questions and measuring the right things. This requires having the right people in governance and developing accountability methods. Without thoughtful partners and leaders from varying levels of the systems and with different perspectives and viewpoints, there may be no way to know or understand how implementation is carried out, what the challenges are, and how to truly measure the systems' impact.

For example, in developing accountability for improving the quality of child care, we need to factor in the stresses and inequities in the system to authentically measure any impact. Otherwise we may not factor in or account for unresolved systemic issues or the things we can't control. We may need to account for larger quality issues such as licensing standards when measuring the impact at the program level. We also need to be realistic about what improvements can be made with the resources available if issues such as compensation, work environment, or benefits cannot be improved.

Therefore, when determining the impact of programs, services, and systems, are we measuring the right things? To be authentic with accountability, we have to ask the right questions:

- Are we measuring the impact on the community?
- Are we using the best assessment tools and those that give us the right information?
- Are we measuring the health and mental health of the providers, children, and families?
- Are we measuring the supports for the system?
- Are we assessing the environment for the employees?
- Are we monitoring the stress levels of those working with children and families?
- Are ECE professionals given the resources and support they need?

For example, efforts to improve child care quality frequently include a focus on the preparation and professional development of the workforce. Yet studies by Marcy Whitebook (2016) and others with the Center for the Study of Child Care Employment (CSCCE) tell us that for those working with children to apply the knowledge and skills they have learned through professional development efforts, a supportive workplace environment is required. Without decent compensation, benefits, planning time, and support, it is hard to improve program quality. In addition, early educators often earn low wages, which can lead to stress from concern about food and housing. Close to half of all early educators in the United States rely on some form of federal income support (Gould, Austin, and Whitebook 2017).

To address these issues, CSCCE researchers developed the Supportive Environment Quality Underlying Adult Learning (SEQUAL) tool. It is used to assess the workplace environment and evaluate how well it supports early learning teaching staff in their work. It is also a way to give voice to these staff and to better understand their working conditions.

Similar to how we might measure the environments for the children's learning, we need to understand the systems that surround us and are part of our work. This provides input from those directly involved in the systems improvement work and who are a critical component and layer of the larger system.

SEQUAL is an example of an authentic assessment tool. As the CSCCE's (accessed 2017) website states, "SEQUAL can assist researchers in understanding the interplay between teacher education, the work environment, and efforts to improve program quality and facilitate children's learning. It can be used by policymakers to inform decision-making and guide resource allocations." It can also "guide improvements to program policies, practices, and relationships." The tool provides a way to look at and measure the underlying issues. It also makes it possible to be more authentic and accountable for program effectiveness along with financial and systemic practices, impacts, and challenges.

Imagine a system where information is gathered from all levels and shared horizontally and vertically across all levels. Then, based on input from each of these levels, decisions are made and goals and support components are developed. This would be a system with authentic accountability. It's not easy work, and it takes time and substantial resources. But a system of this type is incredibly impactful and moves the field forward.

The concept of a well-aligned and authentically informed ECE system, complete with a foundation of adequate funding and resources, is reflected in figure 7.1. In this diagram, each level informs the others, and the system builds on the strong base. Research informs programs, and programs inform research. All the levels also inform each other and are supported by responsive, inclusive, and aligned policies and professional development. All layers of the system lead, inform, and involve families in the support of children's optimal development.

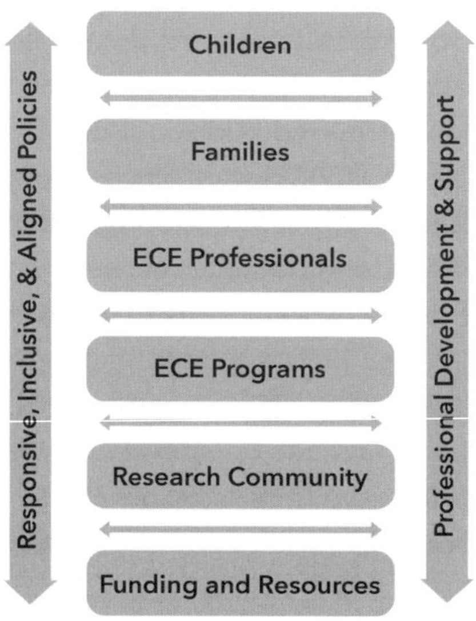

Adapted from Ames 2012.

Developing Leadership Teams

After years of working with leadership teams, Rath and Conchie (2008, 22) stated, "While each member had his or her own unique strengths, the most cohesive and successful teams possessed broader groupings of strengths." The authors suggest that there are four domains of leadership strengths: executing, influencing, relationship building, and strategic thinking.

Those who have strengths in the executing domain know how to get things done. They are achievers and have discipline and focus to work toward a solution. They take responsibility, are deliberate in their actions, and will work tirelessly to achieve a goal.

Those with influencing leadership abilities are strong communicators and will speak up and make sure a message or idea is heard. Rath and Conchie (25) state that influencers are self-assured and that even with few words, their confidence will "project authority and win followers." Influencers get people involved, can rally others around the team's ideas, and convey the significance of the work.

But it is those with relationship-building skills that help build and hold a team together. They are inclusive and bring a positive energy and feeling of connectedness to the group. This fosters a collective spirit and a stronger team, which helps move the team's work forward with a sense of harmony and success.

Leaders with strong strategic-thinking skills keep a team focused on all the possibilities. They like to learn and continuously absorb and analyze new information to help teams make better decisions. Strategic thinkers value ideas and like to figure out future opportunities and directions.

Rath and Conchie say leaders need not possess all these qualities. But strengths in all these domains should be present within the team across its collective members. The authors suggest that "although individuals need not be well-rounded, teams should be" (23). Rath and Conchie add that team members often have strengths in multiple domains. The goal is to find a combination and balance of different strengths and qualities across the team.

Understanding and Acknowledging Power Issues

Power issues will occur in any systems-building work. This is an inherent component and not anything to shy away from, but it is something to understand and work with. Organizations have power, and so do individuals. Acknowledging and understanding your own personal power and the power structures and issues will help effectively build the system, as it helps to know how power can be leveraged and used to move the work forward, make progress, and create change.

Understand Your Own Personal Power

All of us have our own personal power. As leaders, we must understand our approach to power, as well as our issues, challenges, assumptions, and privileges with power. Understanding and developing both your values and comfort levels with issues of power is an important step for you to take. You may have to ask yourself some challenging questions. What is power to you? Do you think you have power? Do you think others do? Why or why not? How do you feel about power? Where did your thoughts and feelings about power come from? What experiences with power have shaped your beliefs?

People often think of power as control over something or someone. But power over others is really dominance or oppression. On the other hand, personal power is the strength within yourself. Gonzalez-Mena (2013, 38) thinks of personal power as "the ability to be who you truly are." We are all born with personal power, the power to make decisions, and control over our own lives and choices. But we also receive a lot of information about power and have many interactions with power, both good and bad, throughout our lives. These messages and experiences affect our ability to tap into our personal power, or even understand it. And every single person's experiences with power are different and influenced by so many things—including socioeconomic status, race, age, gender, family, physical ability, religion, and language, just to name a few. Some members may have experienced an increase in power because of these attributes, while others may have lost power or suffered from an oppressed status. For example, in *Born a Crime: Stories from a South African Childhood*, Trevor Noah recounts the power issues from his childhood in 1980s apartheid South Africa. As a mixed-race child, Noah often had to stay indoors to avoid being seen by authorities. He learned that speaking multiple languages was a form of power. His ability to speak with people in their language gained him acceptance and access, allowing him to move between townships, neighborhoods, and circles of different kids.

Each person will come to the planning process with very different views about leadership and power. Some may consider leadership to be a challenge, threat, or way to obtain greater power. Others may not realize their own personal power in the situation. Effective leaders need to have an understanding of their own personal power as well as the issues possibly surrounding others' feelings and perceptions of power. The goal is to establish a culture of trust, inclusiveness, and respect, where all have the ability to tap into and use their own personal power. When this type of supportive environment and inclusiveness is established, members feel empowered to contribute.

Importance of Power Structures

From the beginning, it is crucial to acknowledge both formal and informal power within the collaborative:

- **Formal power**—Can include formal authority due to institutional powers and positions; control of resources, information, knowledge, or expertise; and control of decision making
- **Informal power**—Can include societal or institutionalized power due to race, class, and age; communication and interpersonal skills; charisma, persuasiveness, and confidence; and the ability to manage change

As you embark on systems-building work, make an effort to learn who is in the room. What organizations are participating? What does each organization do, and what power does it wield? What individuals are engaged in the work? What positions do they hold, and what power or authority do they have in their respective organizations or in the community? What sorts of resources, knowledge, expertise, or skills does each bring to the work? How might that help or hinder the group? Who has more privilege or institutionalized power in the group, and who has less? What can be done to recognize that and mitigate it? Who or what needs to be empowered, and how might this be done?

These are hard questions, but all of them can be discussed openly and transparently. Everyone knows these tough power issues are there, so give voice to them and honor viewpoints, ideas, and feelings about them. Power is a good thing, and it can help accomplish goals and build systems. Power will be used to help make decisions and allocate time and resources. Power can help build alliances, advocate for policy change, and gain stakeholder buy-in. Effective leaders can and should help set the stage and the tone for these conversations.

Roberts (2010) suggests honoring the self-interest of all parties from the onset. All participants in a group will naturally want to protect or promote their own interests or those of their organization. It is essential for all to be clear about individual or organizational needs. When all the organizational interests are clear, then all can begin to determine and work toward the common goals. Sometimes a certain amount of negotiation or accommodation may be necessary to agree on common goals while honoring individual organization missions and needs.

Roberts adds that interests are different than demands or positions. Demands and positions are what people or organizations believe they need or must have. Interests are the underlying reasons, needs, or values behind the position. Focus attention on the interests and find the common needs and values. This will help all work together to identify the interests in common and develop shared goals and vision.

Sharing Power: Ensure an Equitable Playing Field

Wherever and whenever possible, the goal should be to share power. With a commitment to social justice, leadership for ECE systems building must strive to ensure that all have a voice and an equal say. The goal of an effective system is to develop a model for shared power and ensure an equitable playing field for all involved. This is not easy and not always possible, but it should be a goal and a model to strive for.

As we learned from Smith and the Bay Area Early Learning Partnership, it is critical to the success of a collaborative effort to move beyond individual interests and instead focus on the common purpose and issues that are for the greater good of the whole. This requires sharing power and striving for equity. All the time and attention spent on governance, decision-making, problem solving, accountability, relationships, and communication should lead toward this vision of equity and shared power. This part of the work is revolutionary and can transform how organizations and collaborations operate. This can result in systems change that addresses and transcends current challenges.

Part IV

Sustaining the Collaborative Leadership Work

CHAPTER 8

Measuring Progress and Sustaining the Work

WITH SYSTEMS WORK, measuring progress is critical to establishing a track record of reaching goals and achieving outcomes. Tracking progress is essential if we want to know if our work is making a difference and if our efforts are leading to improvement and solving problems. By measuring progress, we can have evidence-based results to tell the story and broadcast success. Measuring progress can provide key information to report to funders and stakeholders and to help build and sustain the work. We can modify program design or structural components using the lessons learned.

Develop a Plan for Continuous Evaluation and Improvement

A major part of measuring progress is having a plan. It's difficult to figure out what to measure, how to continuously gather information, and how to determine what needs changing or improving without knowing what you are planning to achieve and how you plan to do that. Programs should inform the evaluation, and, in return, evaluation should inform program development and design. So developing a plan to both guide the work and continuously measure progress is necessary for ongoing program success. This is when a framework becomes important. It maps out the goals and desired outcomes. It articulates what you plan to measure and what will be the key indicators of success.

A framework can guide the development of an evaluation plan by providing the information on system design, activities, anticipated outcomes, and goals. Use the framework to plan the evaluation activities so the data you collect will be what you need to gauge progress toward outcomes and goals. Determine measurable benchmarks that can quantify the incremental progress of the strategies and activities, leading toward longer-term goals.

Check Progress along the Way

We often think of evaluation as something that happens at the end. But it is critical to check in on the progress toward goals and to gauge the success of the collaborative systems-building efforts along the way. With this information, adjustments can be made to address challenges and determine ways to build on successes. Waiting until later can lead to issues going unnoticed and problems going unresolved. You will reach better outcomes if you have opportunities to fine-tune as you go along.

Discover and Use Lessons Learned

Systems work is ongoing, and there is much to be learned throughout the journey. With the complexities of the process and the multilayered details of the work, there is much to evaluate, measure, reflect on, and analyze. Be open to learning and to discovering things you may not have expected. Lessons learned can be used to improve systems-building efforts and programmatic implementation, guiding the work to greater efficiency and success.

Ensure Accountability

With public and private investments and community support for the work, all stakeholders will want some level of accountability for the work. Accountability will be necessary to be able to demonstrate results. Both state and local systems efforts will need to show the impact of their efforts and justify the investment of funds. For ongoing support, presenting ongoing evidence of lasting impact and long-term benefits of the work will be necessary. This is when it becomes crucial to have thought long and hard about the intended outcomes and how those outcomes will be measured. Measure those things that provide the information needed to tell the story you want to tell. As we learned from the Palm Beach County story, it is important to frame your work around the outcomes you are striving for, how the outcomes will be achieved, and whether the strategies are realistic and measurable.

Systems-building work is complex, with multiple levels, partners, programs, and services. In addition, funding streams and financial structures may be spread across multiple agencies. The administration and governance may also be complex and multilayered. Add to this the complexity of authentic assessment amid social and political pressures, challenges, and inequities, and evaluating systems work becomes even more challenging. To address these complexities, Coffman (2012) suggests measuring systems efforts across five areas:

- **context**—the environment surrounding the system
- **components**—the programs and services of the system
- **connections**—the linkages in the system between organizations, programs, and sectors
- **infrastructure**—the supports of the system
- **scale**—the comprehensive access and inclusion of the system

Each community and system effort will be different based on needs, social and political pressures, contexts, and opportunities. Some systems-building efforts may include all five of these areas and some may not. In addition, there may not be a linear approach to all of these areas. Some collaboratives may work on a few areas at one point in time and on other areas at different times. There may be lesser or greater gains or accomplishments in some areas at different times as well.

For context, measurable systems-level outcomes could be the level of public and political awareness or strength of will surrounding the issues, the progress toward policy changes to affect the system, or increased funding streams and/or levels of funding. Progress on systems components could be measured by gathering data on the number of new programs or services, increased accessibility of programs or services, or improved program quality. Examples of measurable outcomes for connections are increased alignment of services or shared intake and referral systems. Examples of systems-level infrastructure outcomes might be more consistent and/or better-aligned standards or the development of a collaborative governance structure. To measure, the scale will include determining if the number or areas the program intended to reach were served or if the programs and systems are in place to do so.

The Leader's Role

As leaders, our role will be to maintain focus on the bigger vision and model patience and perseverance. Determining methods for assessing and maintaining accountability can be challenging but important work. It will also be imperative to collaborate and maintain trust in the process and the work. Everyone should be involved in determining what accountability processes are put in place to maintain transparency and continue to build and preserve trust. Leaders can help guide the work and ensure a collaborative process to determine which areas can and should be evaluated and how these areas might be measured.

Assess Collaborative Function and Impact of Shared Efforts

Throughout the work, gather information on how the collaboration is going. Maintaining trusting relationships and productive collaborative effort is critical to success. Think of how you could monitor and assess the health and effectiveness of the collaboration. How are the connections and relationships between group members? What are the trust levels among those working on the project? Do all involved have a shared understanding of the vision and goals? Do all agree with the direction the collaborative effort is going? Are there clear decision-making processes? Are the meetings organized and productive? Are you accomplishing your agreed-upon goals?

These questions can help assess if the collaboration is functioning well and working toward success. They are critical to keeping the collaboration healthy. Some say a team or shared effort can only be as strong as its weakest link. If there are weak areas, conflicts of interest, or ways the collaboration is not functioning well, then its overall impact will be reduced or the systems-building efforts could fail. Determine ways to build these questions into the ongoing evaluation of the system and gather information regularly enough to prevent any issues from undermining progress. Adjustments based on information gathered and lessons learned can keep a collaboration running smoothly and facilitate progress.

Gather Feedback on Goals and Benchmarks

To ensure accountability, it is necessary to gather information on the progress made toward your stated goals. It is important for those working on the project as well as those stakeholders watching from the wings to be able to see measurable progress. Gathering feedback on the type and amount of progress made toward stated goals will help you demonstrate results as well as learn what needs changing or adjusting. This will help you establish a track record of achievement while also providing opportunities to try out new ideas, gather feedback on them, and use what you've learned to continue or modify any innovative approaches.

Gathering data during the planning stages provides opportunities to review the information and make decisions throughout the process. For example, after reflecting on five years of development of Missouri's statewide QRIS, Kathy R. Thornburg and Denise Mauzy (2012, 234) concluded that having a pilot or test phase in which to collect data is essential and "allows decision makers to be responsive to certain program issues that can be identified only through actual pilot/implementation activities." Thornburg and Mauzy suggest that this process can lead to stronger and more relevant program models because the feedback on progress toward goals and benchmarks is collected, reflected on, and used.

Determine Needed Changes and Next Steps

Use what you've learned from the information gathered to determine what needs to be changed. What needs to be done differently to reach stated goals? What should be modified to better achieve desired outcomes? It may take stepping away from the problem and using the data to look at things from a different vantage point. Bringing in other group members to take a fresh look from a new perspective may help. Perhaps those working in the programs or those directly involved with system activities will be best able to generate necessary changes.

Determine next steps to address where changes are needed. Don't be afraid to be innovative and try something new. At the same time, try not to make changes that give you such different data that it becomes difficult to measure any progress. Be sure to include how changes will be measured to determine effectiveness. If changes are made too often or components or strategies differ too much, establishing a baseline against which to measure may be challenging. If you are always comparing apples to oranges, building credibility and a record of success may be hard. What's most important is to have a can-do approach to solving problems and addressing challenges as soon as you learn what is working effectively and what is not.

Celebrate and Acknowledge Accomplishments

Recognizing successes along the way is crucial. Take the time to notice and acknowledge accomplishments and celebrate incremental steps achieved. We often get so busy and mired down in the work that we forget to stop and reflect on how far we've actually come. The overall goal may be big, but you will have many opportunities to celebrate small wins as you go.

Celebration builds relationships and maintains motivation. Celebrating together can bring the group closer by sharing the joy that comes with a sense of accomplishment. Celebrating success also helps keep everyone energized for the work. It's exciting to take pride in the progress that has been made. It inspires the group to continue to make strides toward the bigger vision.

Celebrations don't have to be large, costly events. A small gesture can have a big impact. One of my colleagues on a collaborative project gives out little treats such as candy bars to acknowledge both individual and collective accomplishments. At a meeting I was at recently, organizers gave out a pen and water bottle with the agency's name and logo in a nice gift bag. The recipients really liked these and appreciated being acknowledged for their contributions.

People like to be acknowledged and appreciated for their work. As leaders, we should take the time to do so. Acknowledge and celebrate the individual and collective accomplishments and incremental steps that have led to results. Have fun and celebrate the good work!

Sustain the Work

I'm sure many of us have examples of projects we have worked on that were finally going well only to end due to a lack of funds or planning. Planning to sustain the work should start as soon as systems building begins. Systems building should be both a short game and a long game from the onset. While developing all the short-term strategies, activities, programs, and services, thinking ahead about how to sustain all that is being built is critical.

Funding is obviously a key issue. Depending on the funding arrangements for the collaborative, this may need to be a substantial aspect of the work. Programs, services, or even departments or agencies may need to be realigned to maintain funding streams. Each community and state has its own unique funding opportunities and challenges. Some states have undergone significant changes to develop ongoing funding streams for systems-level projects. This work often includes building the political will through advocacy efforts. It can also require fund development, including grant writing and other systems-building components, to develop the funding infrastructure necessary to sustain the work.

Beyond funding, leadership is needed to sustain systems. The systems effort will succeed or fail depending on how the collaboration is positioned to sustain itself. Like other entities, collaborative efforts will continue on in healthy ways with ongoing investment. Effective collaborations require ongoing attention, nurturing, support, and work. Paying attention to these key leadership needs will greatly benefit and enhance ongoing systems-level work.

And remember, leadership does not mean that one single leader has to know everything. In fact, I think great leaders know themselves well and recognize what they understand and when they need information and expertise from others. Knowing when to ask for help or more information is a strength, not a weakness. Great leaders seek out others with the knowledge, skills, and expertise needed to successfully accomplish the work at hand. If you need knowledge or skills to understand funding streams or economic efficiencies, opportunities, and challenges, seek out those who can help provide this information. If evaluation methods or data systems are not your area of expertise, then find those who possess this knowledge and can contribute their wisdom to the collaborative team.

To sustain the system, you may have to ask yourselves some hard questions. A leader's role may be to help the group reflect on some challenging issues to determine the best options and plan for sustainability. Here are some questions you might need to consider:

- Do you have the right structure?
    - Are the right partners involved?
    - Do you have the necessary staffing model?
    - Do you have the best governance arrangement?
- What have you accomplished?
    - Do you have anything to show from your work?
    - Do you have sufficient stories to tell and data to share?
    - Are the programs or services making enough of a difference?
    - Has the work led to greater efficiencies, increased alignment, or more streamlined programs and services?
    - Is there anything unique or significant about what you have achieved?
- What needs to change?
    - Are there aspects of the system that don't work or need improving?
    - Are any components duplicative?
    - Could anything be more cost-effective?

Answering some or all of these questions will help gauge project success to date. It will also help make any necessary improvements to better position the organization for potential funding.

Identify the Leaders and Vision Champions

To sustain the work, determine who among you has the vision to carry it forward. Identify the leaders who are the champions for the work. You may need several vision leaders—champions across sectors, agencies, levels, and programs. Look to those who believe in the work and those who are gaining the respect of the collaborative members. Consider both those members who are the most vocal and those who tend to be quiet and in the background but are steadfast champions of the project and understand the significance of the work.

Sustain the Collaboration

To sustain the collaboration and keep it running smoothly, consistent and focused attention is required. The collaboration itself, comprised of the different partner organizations and members, is a critical component of the work. The collaboration is the foundation for all the work. That foundation must stay strong, or, like any other structure, it will begin to crumble.

Part of the leader's work is to keep a watchful eye over the bigger picture and foundation pieces. Sometimes leadership is part champion for the project, part guardian of the process and work, and part caretaker of the system and structures themselves. Leaders can provide the attention, awareness, and persistence needed to hold the collaboration together.

To sustain the collaboration, leaders should focus on the following areas:

- **Relationships**—So much of the collaboration is the relationships it is built on. And just like all the other relationships in our lives, a collaborative needs work and attention. Nurture the relationships and find ways to maintain a sense of community and cohesion among group members. If new people join the collaborative, take steps to build positive relationships between the new and existing members. Then keep up the team-building work even after the group has gotten to know each other. This will deepen relationships and give the collaboration strength, allowing its members to tackle challenges together.
- **Trust**—As a leader, you must build and maintain others' trust in you as well as be the guardian and caretaker of the group's trust in each other. This helps maintain an honest and open process. Trust in the collaboration can start to erode if group members think their opinions aren't valued. So effective collaborative leaders are vigilant in ensuring all viewpoints and ideas are welcomed and respected.
- **Common vision and goals**—Ongoing buy-in, commitment to a common vision, and dedication to the collective goals keep a collaboration

healthy and strong. Continually check in to see if the common vision and goals are still holding the group together. Determine if goals need to be changed or modified to reflect shifts or adjustments in the overall vision. For example, after several years of work and reflection on implementation, data, and outcomes, you may find it necessary to make adjustments based on what you've learned. Going through this process together can be a great exercise. It can keep the collaboration vital and energized, allowing the group to reflect, recommit to the existing vision and goals, or brainstorm collectively on any needed revisions. However, while it's okay or even necessary to revisit the goals as a group from time to time, you don't want to get into a habit of changing them too frequently. Doing so can cause the collaboration to lose focus and momentum.

- **Shared purpose**—A collaborative must continually maintain agreement on its shared purpose. The group can lose steam if the inspiration and drive to persevere becomes unclear or less focused. If people lose sight completely of the reasons for working together, keeping the collaboration going may become difficult. Without continued understanding of the common goals, group members may feel frustrated and lose interest in participating. For the collaboration to continually thrive, members must share an understanding of the purpose of their work. A leader's role is to keep checking in to determine the level of agreement and commitment to the purpose.

Put Structures in Place to Keep the System Together

We need to make sure the key support structures are in place and sturdy, just as we would for a building, if we want a collaborative to remain standing. With any systems-building effort, a fair amount of glue is needed between all the pieces to hold it all together. To sustain the collaborative, make sure these systems are clearly defined and operating as smoothly as possible. Financial structures are critical for ongoing fiscal health. Management, supervision, and staffing structures are vital to maintaining operations and sustaining services and programs. And two structures I consider crucial to the collaborative system itself are communication and governance:

- **Communication structures**—Good communication is vital to any healthy collaboration. If communication breaks down, it will be hard to keep track of the work and maintain the systems-building efforts. Strong communication is a key piece to sustainability. Collaboration can be complicated work with many layers and lots of moving parts. Having structures in place so that everyone involved is aware of what is going on will help ensure the collaborative work stays coherent and strong. Good communication also helps maintain trust. Poor communication or a lack of information can lead to misunderstandings and confusing or even incorrect implementation processes. Establish communication procedures and structures and check often to make sure they are working. Confirm that everyone is getting necessary information in a timely manner and that everyone has clear ways of passing along information to others. This will maintain trust and help sustain the collaboration.

- **Governance**—The oversight and leadership structures of the system are a significant aspect of sustainability. The systems must be able to ensure accountability and continue to operate effectively and efficiently. Having a structure in place that allows members to continue to make decisions and establish and maintain policies will help the collaboration thrive. To manage the system, the governance structure of the collaboration must remain viable and credible. This will ensure that finances and resources are managed well, the system remains healthy and functioning, outcomes are being achieved, and the vision is being realized. It will also help ensure that all members maintain faith in the systems work and continue to persevere toward the long-term goals and bigger mission of the collaboration. To achieve success, all must have confidence that the system is managed well and can survive whatever may happen. This is the definition of sustainability.

Provide Leadership Support

A system needs strong leaders. Leaders in turn need support to keep the collaboration healthy and strong. So it is crucial for the sustainability of the collaboration to have support for those in leadership roles. Leadership can be hard work. Knowing that the collaborative members support and believe in him or her encourages a leader. Find opportunities to reinforce leaders in their roles. This support might take the form of structural components, such as accessible meetings held at convenient locations and times. Ensuring that communication structures allow leaders to get the information they need in a timely manner will also help support their roles.

Supporting leaders can also include letting them know they are making a difference. Leaders are inspired when they have opportunities to see the results of their efforts. Consider building in ways for leaders to hear from others that the work matters. Find ways for staff throughout the system to give input and feedback. Provide opportunities for participants to tell their stories of how this work has benefited them personally. These are often the reasons that leaders get into this work to begin with. It's not about getting credit or a pat on the back but about making things better for those receiving the services or improving conditions for those working in the system.

I have a member of my staff who tells me that she is able to do her job well because she knows I'm taking care of the systems-building leadership and vision work. My efforts provide ways for her to focus on the details of her job and excel at her part of the project. Each of us has a key role, and she reminds me that I'm needed and appreciated in mine. Hearing this inspires and reenergizes me for the hard work ahead. Often this support is all I need to keep going.

Leaders also need opportunities to learn and grow. No one person knows all there is to know, but leaders need to stay current on relevant topics and issues. Providing opportunities to learn from others can help supply new information and keep things fresh and interesting. Perhaps you can bring in guest speakers to present new ideas at meetings or arrange learning sessions with other leaders or groups. Another option might be to build in time to read, research, or reflect on information to provide opportunities to learn something new. Going to conferences or attending meetings with experts or other leaders may also afford new insight or ideas. Not only will this support keep leaders engaged in their own learning, but it can also energize them for future work and inspire them to lead with renewed purpose.

Build Future Leaders

To continue the work for years to come, we must cultivate and sustain effective leaders. As we know, leadership for collaborative systems efforts requires sophisticated skills. Therefore, it is essential to identify and support leaders from within the system and work to nurture their skill building along the way. Be on the lookout for those who begin to take an interest or assume some level of leadership. Provide guidance and assistance to encourage their ongoing leadership development.

Additionally, leadership may be needed in different ways and at different levels. At the board level, for instance, some leadership development training on governance may be necessary. Other emerging leaders may need training or mentoring on communication strategies, conflict resolution, meeting facilitation, or techniques for building a shared vision. It is important to be realistic about how many people with leadership skills are needed and the breadth of knowledge and understanding necessary to sustain the work.

CHAPTER 9

Have Fun and Enjoy the Journey

LEADERSHIP IS A JOURNEY. Often it has no concrete beginning and no definitive end. It is something we do and a role we take on at different points throughout our life and career. And it is frequently a winding path with twists and turns. There will be good days and bad. There will be obvious choices and difficult decisions. And there will be times when you can see the difference you are making and other times when the whole situation seems about as clear as mud. But you are on your way. And you are making a difference, even if only in your immediate surroundings.

When I teach college courses and the students are overwhelmed by the challenges facing them at work or by larger and seemingly insurmountable systemic issues in the field, I remind them that they are already growing, learning, and taking steps to change their corner of the world. Sometimes leadership happens in tiny steps—in fact, sometimes it can take years to see change. But your leadership matters, and you are needed, so find ways to keep at it.

Take Care of Yourself as a Leader

Leadership can be hard work. Find ways to take care of yourself both professionally and personally. I continue to learn and grow, but here are some things I've discovered along the way that help me to continue on my leadership journey.

Be Good to Yourself

As leaders we can become engrossed in all we are working on. I sometimes find it hard to stop working or to leave my work at the office. Long days and difficult projects can leave us tired and stressed. Be good to yourself and recognize when you need to take a break and rest. You can be a more effective leader if you keep your stress level down. Do things that are just for you so you can take care of yourself physically and emotionally. Take a walk, get enough sleep, eat a good meal, watch a movie, spend time with friends, or do whatever activities help you get the rest you need to rejuvenate yourself.

Learn Something New

Sullivan (2016, 175) reminds us that leaders must "Refresh! Renew! Research! Refocus!" She says, "Effective leaders know that even the greatest vision requires updating." It is important to step back, reflect, take in new information, listen to a different perspective, or look at things with fresh eyes. Think of how energizing it is to learn something new or take on a new challenge. Leaders need time and ways to find their growth edge and stay invigorated by their work. Think about what you haven't tried, what more you could do, what else you could learn, or what else you could consider. These ideas will help you continue to grow professionally and stay energized by your leadership.

Surround Yourself with Good People

Challenging situations or people can be draining. Surround yourself with people who help sustain you, energize you, and remind you to take care of yourself. When feeling stressed, take time to be with people who make you feel good. Having mentors or peers who can provide support is also important. Find people to talk to who understand your work or your leadership role. They know what it's like and can help provide perspective, ideas, support, and guidance. Sometimes we just need to think out loud or vent, so having people in your life with good listening skills can help you reflect and keep you grounded in your own strengths.

Maintain Your Integrity

You will be sustained and nurtured by staying true to your core beliefs and values. But doing so is not always easy. However, it is more draining to give up, give in, let go, or be insincere or dishonest about who you are and what you stand for. You may, from time to time, have to let go of circumstances you can't change, but you can continue to maintain your values throughout.

Recognizing what you can and can't influence and choosing your battles wisely is a strength and can be done from a place of integrity. But stay open to learning and know that values can change with new information. Stay flexible and open to possibilities. The key is to take the time to reflect and approach opportunities with a sense of purpose and integrity to do the best by others and yourself.

Find the Humor and Keep Going

I tend to be the person in a meeting who finds the humor in a situation. I like to laugh and enjoy seeing the comedy in things. Some things are just funny! But more than that, if I find the humor and share it out loud, this often helps people relax and ultimately improves the meeting. People are more willing to build relationships, find common ground, and work together to create a shared vision if they are having fun and enjoying the process. Find the joy, because life and work should be fun. We wouldn't want children to be in classrooms where there is never any joy or fun in learning. We shouldn't want that for ourselves or our colleagues either.

Think back on the classes you liked the most, or the work situations or meetings you enjoyed. Now think about why you enjoyed them. I find that the situations I remember most or got the most out of were those in which I felt connected and cared about, in which I was really interested in what was happening, or that were just plain fun. So put on some music, get up and dance, laugh about something, give out candy bars, and whoop it up a little.

Life is short. Have fun and enjoy the journey!

References

Alameda County. 2016. "Alameda County's Emerging Leaders Fellowship in Early Care and Education: A Professional Development Opportunity to Achieve Racial Equity and Systems Change." Acgov.org. www.acgov.org/ece/documents/EmergingLeadersFellowshipApplication.pdf.

Ames, Gretchen. 2015. "Making Voice Visible: A Scholarly Personal Narrative Study Examining the Increasing Pressure for Accountability and Quality Improvement in Early Childhood Education and How It Impacted One Educator's Sense of Agency and Professionalism." PhD diss. Mills College, Oakland, CA.

Arsenault, Jane. 1998. *Forging Nonprofit Alliances.* Washington, DC: The National Alliance for Nonprofit Management and Jossey-Bass.

Bay Area Quality Early Learning Partnership. 2015. "Race to the Top—Early Learning Challenge: Achievements and Lessons Learned from Regional QRIS Implementation." Bay Area Quality Early Learning Partnership. www.bayareaqualitypartnership.com/wp-content/uploads/2016/02/Race-to-the-Top-Early-Learning-Challenge-Achievements.pdf.

Bruner, Charles, Child and Family Policy Center, and The BUILD Initiative. 2017. "A Framework for State Leadership and Action in Building the Components of an Early Childhood System." BUILD Initiative. www.buildinitiative.org/Portals/0/Uploads/Documents/Four_Ovals_paper.pdf.

Bruno, Holly Elissa. 2012. *What You Need to Lead an Early Childhood Program: Emotional Intelligence in Practice*. Washington, DC: NAEYC.

Bruno, Holly Elissa, Janet Gonzalez-Mena, Luis Antonio Hernandez, and Debra Ren-Etta Sullivan. 2013. *Learning from the Bumps in the Road: Insights from Early Childhood Leaders*. St. Paul, MN: Redleaf Press.

California Child Care Resource and Referral Network. 2015. "2015 Child Care Portfolio." California Child Care Resource & Referral Network. www.rrnetwork.org/child_care_data.

Center for the Study of Child Care Employment. 2014. "Supportive Environmental Quality Underlying Adult Learning (SEQUAL)." Center for the Study of Child Care Employment. http://cscce.berkeley.edu/sequal.

Child Care Resource Center. 2017. *Healthy Habits Learned Early in Life: Cultivating Child Care Leaders to Improve Nutrition and Physical Activity*. Los Angeles: Choose Health LA Child Care.

Children's Services Council Palm Beach County. 2017. "Community Learning Visit: Strong Minds." PowerPoint presented at LA QRIS Architects Learning Journey, Palm Beach, FL.

Clifford, Dean. 2012. "Local-Level System Building." In *Early Childhood Systems: Transforming Early Learning*, edited by Sharon Lynn Kagan and Kristie Kauerz, 155–70. New York: Teachers College Press.

Coffman, Julia. 2012. "Evaluating System-Building Efforts." In *Early Childhood Systems: Transforming Early Learning*, edited by Sharon Lynn Kagan and Kristie Kauerz, 199–215. New York: Teachers College Press.

Coleman, Jeanine, and Jodi Hardin. 2012. "Establishing a Common Vision for Colorado's Early Childhood System." In *Early Childhood Systems: Transforming Early Learning*, edited by Sharon Lynn Kagan and Kristie Kauerz, 219–25. New York: Teachers College Press.

Dutton, Jane E., and Gretchen M. Spreitzer, eds. 2014. *How to Be a Positive Leader: Small Actions, Big Impact*. San Francisco: Berrett-Koehler Publishers.

Early Childhood Colorado Framework. 2017. "Early Childhood Colorado Framework: A Shared Vision." Early Childhood Colorado Framework. http://earlychildhoodframework.org/wp-content/uploads/2015/08/ECLC-FRMWRK-062415-LORES.pdf.

First 5 Santa Clara County. 2017. "The Bay Area Quality Rating and Improvement System (QRIS) Partnership." First 5 Santa Clara County. www.first5kids.webflow.io/early-learning/the-bay-area-quality-rating-and-improvement-system.

Goffin, Stacie G. 2013. *Early Childhood Education for a New Era: Leading for Our Profession*. New York: Teachers College Press.

———. 2015. *Professionalizing Early Childhood Education as a Field of Practice: A Guide to the Next Era*. St. Paul, MN: Redleaf Press.

Goffin, Stacie G., and Valora Washington. 2007. *Ready or Not: Leadership Choices in Early Care and Education*. New York: Teachers College Press.

Gonzalez-Mena, Janet. 2013. "Finding Your Personal Power." In *Learning from the Bumps in the Road: Insights from Early Childhood Leaders* by Holly Elissa Bruno, Janet Gonzalez-Mena, Luis Antonio Hernandez, and Debra Ren-Etta Sullivan, 37–40. St. Paul, MN: Redleaf Press.

Gould, Elise, Lea J. E. Austin, and Marcy Whitebook. 2017. *What Does Good Child Care Reform Look Like?* Economic Policy Institute. http://cscce.berkeley.edu/files/2017/03/What-does-good-child-care-reform-look-like.pdf.

HarvardEducation. 2016. "Dean James Ryan's 5 Essential Questions in Life." YouTube. www.youtube.com/watch?v=bW0NguMGIbE.

Kagan, Sharon Lynn. 2015. "Conversations on Early Learning: Building Early Childhood Systems." Houghton Mifflin Harcourt. *Shaped* (blog). www.hmhco.com/blog/building-early-childhood-systems.

Kagan, Sharon Lynn, and Kristie Kauerz, eds. 2012. *Early Childhood Systems: Transforming Early Learning*. New York: Teachers College Press.

Kagan, Sharon Lynn, Kate Tarrant, and Kristie Kauerz. 2012. "Planning an Early Childhood System: Policies and Principles Matter." In *Early Childhood Systems: Transforming Early Learning*, edited by Sharon Lynn Kagan and Kristie Kauerz, 137–54. New York: Teachers College Press.

Kaser, Joyce, Susan Mundry, Katherine E. Stiles, and Susan Loucks-Horsley. 2006. *Leading Every Day: 124 Actions for Effective Leadership*. 2nd ed. Thousand Oaks, CA: Corwin Press.

Kidsdata.org. 2017. "Availability of Child Care for Potential Demand." Lucile Packard Foundation for Children's Health. http://www.kidsdata.org/topic/99/childcareavailability/table#fmt=262&loc=2,127,347,1763,331,348,336,171,321,345,357,332,324,369,358,362,360,337,327,364,356,217,353,328,354,323,352,320,339,334,365,343,330,367,344,355,366,368,265,349,361,4,273,59,370,326,333,322,341,338,350,342,329,325,359,351,363,340,335&tf=79&ch=1247,1248&sortColumnId=0&sortType=asc.

Kouzes, James, and Barry Posner. 2012. *The Leadership Challenge: How to Make Extraordinary Things Happen in Organizations*. San Francisco: The Leadership Challenge.

Kraemer, Harry M. Jansen, Jr. 2011. *From Values to Action: The Four Principles of Values-Based Leadership*. San Francisco: Jossey-Bass.

Lambert, Linda, Deborah Walker, Diane P. Zimmerman, Joanne E. Cooper, Morgan Dale Lambert, Mary E. Gardner, and Margaret Szabo. 2002. *The Constructivist Leader*. 2nd ed. New York: Teachers College Press.

Linden, Russell M. 2002. *Working Across Boundaries: Making Collaboration Work in Government and Nonprofit Organizations*. San Francisco: Jossey-Bass.

Marotz, Lynn R., and Amy Lawson. 2007. *Motivational Leadership in Early Childhood Education*. Clifton Park, NY: Thomson Delmar Learning.

Mattessich, Paul W., Marta Murray-Close, Barbara R. Monsey, and Wilder Research Center. 2001. *Collaboration: What Makes It Work*. St. Paul, MN: Fieldstone Alliance.

Noah, Trevor. 2016. *Born a Crime: Stories from a South African Childhood*. New York: Spiegel & Grau.

Oregon Department of Education. 2016. *Oregon's Quality Rating and Improvement System (QRIS) Revision*. http://5c2cabd466efc6790a0a-6728e7c952118b70f16620a9fc754159.r37.cf1.rackcdn.com/cms/QRIS_Revision_One-pager_Timeline_3303.pdf.

Partners for Children South L.A. 2017. https://partners4childrensla.org.

Rath, Tom, and Barry Conchie. 2008. *Strengths Based Leadership: Great Leaders, Teams, and Why People Follow*. New York: Gallup Press.

Ricci, Ron, and Carl Wiese. 2011. *The Collaboration Imperative: Executive Strategies for Unlocking Your Organization's True Potential*. San Jose, CA: Cisco Systems.

Roberts, Joan M. 2004. *Alliances, Coalitions and Partnerships: Building Collaborative Organizations.* Gabriola Island, BC: New Society Publishers.

———. 2010. *Governance for Collaboratives: A Guide to Resolving Power and Conflict Issues.* Toronto: Joan Roberts Consulting.

Rosen, Evan. 2007. *The Culture of Collaboration: Maximizing Time, Talent and Tools to Create Value in the Global Economy.* San Francisco: Red Ape Publishing.

Rosenow, Nancy. 2016. "Heart-Centered Leadership." In *The Art of Leadership: Leading Early Childhood Organizations*, edited by Bonnie Neugebauer and Roger Neugebauer, 17–20. Redmond, WA: Exchange Press.

Schumacher, Rachel. 2011. "The Early Childhood Systems Working Group—Updating the Ovals: A Guide for Our Rationale." BUILD Initiative. www.buildinitiative.org/Portals/0/Uploads/Documents/Updating_the_Ovals_Guide_to_Rationale.pdf.

Stebbins, Helene M. 2012. "How Do We Get There from Here? Financing the Transformation from a Collection of Programs to an Early Childhood System." In *Early Childhood Systems: Transforming Early Learning*, edited by Sharon Lynn Kagan and Kristie Kauerz, 171–82. New York: Teachers College Press.

Straus, David. 2002. *How to Make Collaboration Work: Powerful Ways to Build Consensus, Solve Problems, and Make Decisions.* San Francisco: Berrett-Koehler Publishers.

Sullivan, Debra R. 2016. "Spreading the Wealth: Leadership at All Levels." In *The Art of Leadership: Leading Early Childhood Organizations*, edited by Bonnie Neugebauer and Roger Neugebauer, 34–37. Redmond, WA: Exchange Press.

Sykes, Maurice. 2014. *Doing the Right Thing for Children: Eight Qualities of Leadership*. St. Paul, MN: Redleaf Press.

Tamm, James W., and Ronald J. Luyet. 2004. *Radical Collaboration: Five Essential Skills to Overcome Defensiveness and Build Successful Relationships.* New York: HarperCollins.

Thornburg, Kathy R., and Denise Mauzy. 2012. "The Missouri Quality Rating System." In *Early Childhood Systems: Transforming Early Learning*, edited by Sharon Lynn Kagan and Kristie Kauerz, 232–38. New York: Teachers College Press.

Whitebook, M., E. King, G. Philipp, and L. Sakai. 2016. *Teachers' Voices: Work Environment Conditions That Impact Teacher Practice and Program Quality.* Berkeley: Center for the Study of Child Care Employment, University of California, Berkeley.

Winer, Michael, and Karen Ray. 1994. *Collaboration Handbook: Creating, Sustaining, and Enjoying the Journey.* St. Paul, MN: Amherst H. Wilder Foundation.

Wold and Associates, 2011. *Partners in Pandemic and Emergency Readiness: Building a Public Health System of Response with Child Care Networks in Los Angeles County.* Los Angeles: County of Los Angeles Department of Public Health.

Work Group for Community Health and Development at the University of Kansas. 2017. "Section 1: Strategies for the Long-Term Sustainability of an Initiative: An Overview." Community Tool Box. http://ctb.ku.edu/en/table-of-contents/sustain/long-term-sustainability/overview/main.

Index